I0147525

LIVES REMEMBERED

A Memoir

ALSO BY LINDA TY-CASPER

The Transparent Sun (Short Stories), Peso Books, 1963.

The Peninsulars (Historical Novel), Bookmark, 1964.

The Secret Runner (Short Stories), Florentino/National Book, 1974.

The Three-Cornered Sun (Historical Novel), New Day, 1979; Exploding Galaxies, 2024.

Dread Empire (Historical Novel), Heinemann, 1980.

Hazards of Distance (Historical Novel), New Day, 1981.

Fortress in the Plaza (Historical Novel), New Day, 1985.

Awaiting Trespass: A Pasion (Historical Novel), Readers International, 1985; New Day, 1989.

Wings of Stone (Historical Novel), Readers International, 1986; New Day, 1990.

Ten Thousand Seeds (Historical Novel), Ateneo de Manila University Press, 1987.

A Small Party in a Garden (Historical Novel), New Day, 1988.

Common Continent: Selected Stories, Ateneo de Manila University Press, 1991.

Kulasyon: Uninterrupted Vigils (First Chapters), Giraffe, 1995.

DreamEden (Historical Novel), Ateneo de Manila University Press, 1996; Washington University Press, 1997.

The Stranded Whale (Historical Novel), Giraffe, 2002.

A River, One-Woman Deep: Stories, PALH, 2017; University of Santo Tomas Publishing House 2018

Will You Happen, Past the Silence, Through the Dark?: Remembering Leonard Ralph Casper (Biography), PALH 2022; Ateneo de Manila University Press, 2023.

LIVES REMEMBERED

A Memoir

LINDA TY-CASPER

LIVES REMEMBERED
A MEMOIR
By Linda Ty-Casper

Copyright © 2025 by Linda Ty-Casper

All rights reserved. No part of this book may be
reproduced or distributed in any form or by any means,
or stored in a database or retrieval system, without prior
written permission.

Published by PALH
(Philippine American Literary House)
PO Box 5099
Santa Monica, CA 90409, USA
PALHBOOKS.com; palh@aol.com

Library of Congress Control Number: 2024920559

ISBN: 978-1-953716-46-0 (Paperback)
ISBN: 978-1-953716-47-7 (Hardcover)
ISBN: 978-1-953716-48-4 (Ebook)

THIS BOOK IS DEDICATED TO

Francisco Figueroa Ty

Catalina Velasquez-Ty

CONTENTS

PART 1: Starting

PART 2: Grants and Conferences/Readings/Talks

Portrait of Blas Viardo (adult),
great-grandfather of Linda Ty-Casper)

Portrait of Florencia Paez Viardo (adult),
great-grandmother of Linda Ty-Casper

PART 1

STARTING

EARLY MEMORIES

My earliest memories are of seeing my younger sister Baby falling down the stairs, asking for "Sang peya, bayot pepa"; of Nanay, our grandmother, inside the kolongkolong, reading *Liwayway* while Baby sat outside the playpen; of my holding tightly to a bag of peanuts at the Mehan Garden, while the elephant, its trunk high over me, waited for me to feed it.

With a blue Kodak my father took a picture of me playing piko, my shadow on the sidewalk; of my mother wearing a saya instead of her usual dress, holding Baby who is watching me crying at our mother's knee; of Tio Osong Velasquez who came in a shiny new car to bring me a doll almost as big as myself when he won the Sweepstakes. He named his daughter Linda. So did Tio Miling Viardo. I was their first niece.

We lived in an accessoria on Camarines Street, a few meters from the main gate of the Manila Jockey Club. Just outside its fence was the stable owned by Mang Terio. One afternoon instead of taking a nap, I went into the stalls, past the sotas, my slippers sinking in the sawdust, but quickly ran out when a horse stuck its head through the opening above the feed pail, to nibble at my hair.

Between the stable and our accessoria was the Dionisio's apartment. Mr. Dionisio wrote for Tagalog newspapers, and also, for *Liwayway*. A nationalist, he named his son Araw. When the family bought a piano, Mrs. Dionisio suggested I take lessons with Araw who had started playing simple tunes. I came a few times. Too impatient to learn, I just moved my fingers over the keys the way the teacher did before our lessons: but making noise, not music. Mrs. Dionisio just smiled, and never told on me.

At the corner was a store tended by Ima who was old, short, dark and barefoot; a sleeve of her loose baro drooping over one shoulder. Her son, Custodio, resembled the owner of the accessorias. Ima stood behind the candy counter, though she sometimes fell asleep in the wooden chair against the wall. Whenever I had a centavo, I ran to the store for lemon drops. Ima always gave me an extra candy, putting different colors on a piece of paper, then twisting the top before handing it to me. I waited till I got home before I opened the bag, to count them again.

At night, a man with a turban came with a stool on which to sit just outside Ima's store, keeping watch until morning; his white garment some kind of light shadow. I felt safe seeing him there, when I looked out.

I was not supposed to, but sometimes I left Ima's store by the door on Felix Huertas to see if a girl, my age, was sitting at their doorstep. That meant her father, an American, was home and she could play outside until he called her in.

Across from Ima's store was the Alzate house. Of concrete, it was large with wide windows. The stone fence had iron grilles. Once a week a dog trainer, wearing leather boots, came to teach tricks to their German shepherd. We never crossed over to that side of Camarines since there was no sidewalk.

Morning and afternoon, ice drop and ice cream vendors came with their carts, bells ringing. Balancing bilaos piled with kakanin on their heads, women vendors walked up and down Camarines. Ate Luz waited for the one selling spiced cowries which she pulled out from their shells with a long pin. Afternoons, the taho vendor came carrying two pails on a pole across his shoulders. We could have taho so we would run home to get our own glasses. We were not to use those soaking in the vendor's pail. Some days a man came by to clean people's ear, using very tiny silver spoons to scoop out the wax. This was just for grown-ups.

On May nights, there were Santacruzans with sagalas costumed as personages from the Bible. On either side, people walked holding candles, singing. I closed my eyes when Judith came by, carrying the bloody head of John the Baptist. Neighborhoods competed for the longest procession, the prettiest sagalas and the most elaborate costumes. Sometimes there were several processions and the chanting from other streets merged like rain. Sometimes the procession was short, a few children and parents with small candles.

Sundays, horse races were held at the Jockey Club. Camarines would then be crowded with aficionados and food vendors. Occasionally, Lola Salud Policarpio, Nanay's younger sister would bring a kaing of lanzones, sit outside our door while I called out to passersby. At the end of the day, she gave me what was left in the kaing, usually the bubut. She had two

3

sons, Tio Onching and Tio Uling. For years we exchanged visits with their children, and grandchildren.

During the year, colleges and universities held programs and dances at the Jockey Club. I could stay up late to watch women students in long gowns walk by with their escorts. Some had little tiaras on their heads. I wanted to grow up and wear those crowns.

On Sunday, people walked up to the Church of the Holy Ghost on Avenida Rizal, the other end of Camarines. A tranvia went up and down the Avenida, passing Ang Tibay Shoes and the old Opera House, to Santa Cruz where there was another church; and a bridge across the Pasig River to Intramuros. That was a different world from Camarines.

NANAY/GABRIELA PAEZ VIARDO

I nside a gold trimmed portamoneda tucked between the sayas in her aparador, Nanay kept her baptismal certificate, dated 1871. Her mother, was Florencia Paez, from Malabon; her father Blas Viardo/Biardo who had red hair and came from Portugal. He owned a carriage, the right reserved for Spaniards. Nanay said, Blas' hand touched Florencia's hand when he gave her the handkerchief she had dropped; and for her to keep her honor, he had to marry her. Kuya Roddy Dulay found a Gaspar Viardo in the registry of property in Pasig, Rizal. Also from Lisbon, Gaspar owned most of a town of Tanyong according to Ate Cording. Tina's friend in Sacramento who is a research librarian, Meredith Sarmento, found a few Viardo connections, but not directly between Blas and Gaspar. I remember visiting Tio Doring in the farmacia across from the Church of San Bartolome. His daughter Conchita taught at St. James Academy.

Agrifina/Pinang, Nanay's second daughter, gave me two family portraits, over a hundred years old. Long ago, itinerant artists peddled partly finished portraits in the provinces, and clients chose the frame on which to have their likeness painted. Both Florencia Paez and Blas Viardo were seated; Florencia with the oldest daughter Kikay; Blas with the oldest son, Crispulo or Crispin. Tia Pinang found the portraits in the silong of a relative's house, covered with poultry droppings. After taking out the rings, earrings, necklaces and jeweled buttons, the relative apparently lost all interest. In 1974 when I was a Radcliffe institute Fellow—Fellows were considered officers of Harvard with special privileges—at Rod Perez's suggestion, we took the faded portraits to Gerry Cohen at the Fogg art museum to have the bukbuk holes filled in and the portraits preserved.

Nanay's older sister, Francisca/Kikay, married a Viardo; a first cousin who was a general in the Spanish army. Kikay studied in Manila, but Nanay would not leave San Isidro so never learned to speak Castilian Spanish. However, she learned the Pasion by heart and was allowed by the parroco to prepare the servants for confession and Communion. During Lent, Nanay told stories from the Pasion. The Apostles John and James were called Sons of Thunder—Boanerges. The word had the sound of thunderbolts.

Nanay married Lucio Velasquez from Cabiao and Macabebe, a master tailor. Their house in San Isidro was across from that of Blas, her father. One morning, Don Blas called out from his window that the barber was on his way to her house. The next instant she saw him collapse, and die. Not long after, her husband Lucio passed away. There is a photograph of his coffin with Nanay and all her seven children around it. Catalina, the youngest, was in the arms of Agrifina.

One year, while a typhoon raged, Nanay dreamed of the three children she had left at her brother's house. Without waiting for the storm to abate, she hired a banquero to take her across the flooded Rio Grande, and found out that all three—Pacita, Ambrosio, Rufino—had died of typhus; had been made to pasture carabaos, to sleep with servants instead of in the house.

After her house burned down, Nanay suddenly left San Isidro with her four daughters. With no clear idea of how far Manila was, where she would stay, Nanay hired a carromata. On the way, they were stopped by bandits who recognized Nanay from the smallpox scars on her nose. "That's the daughter of Don Blas," the leader said, letting them go.

Finally reaching Manila, Nanay met a first cousin who brought them to a house in Intramuros, paying the rent for them. He also introduced her to the gambling house where he and other cousins played monte. Such houses were open only to friends. Thereafter, Nanay was welcome at the gaming tables. She must not have played monte; more likely, panguingue. When she did not have the capital, the owners advanced her puhunan, knowing her cousins would vouch for her. By Nanay's account, she always won, and was able to start supporting her family by herself.

I don't recall who that first cousin was. I know Jose Paez was a first cousin. Also Dr. Jose Albert who was, I found out when I was doing research for *The Peninsulars*, a member of the first Philippine Commission under the Americans. I remember him coming in a calesa/quelis to Camarines, when we were sick; wearing the white de hilo suit which government officials wore, and telling Fidela to open the capiz windows, which she closed immediately as soon as he left. I recall Tia

Pinang taking me to visit his house, near Azcarraga, where the central market now stands. Large trees provided shade all day. During the Liberation of Manila, bombshells penetrated the cover of trees, hitting both Lolo Jose and Lola Loleng. They were buried under the sampaloc tree.

Gabriela Paez Viardo

NANAY'S DAUGHTERS

From intramuros, Nanay moved to Callejon de la Fe, behind the Quiapo church. On her brother's invitation, she moved again, this time to live with his family on Felix Huertas. When new accesorias were built on Camarines, Nanay rented one--number 604--but continued to visit her brother until his house, and others on Felix Huertas, were razed and the Manila Jockey Club built on the cleared land. I recall Nanay saying that after he became ill, he asked her to come every day to make him soup, reminding her to look under his pillow after he passed. Someone, however, beat Nanay to what he had intended for her.

By this time, Nanay's daughters had taken over providing for the family. Nanay stopped playing panguingue. Fidela, my Godmother so I called her Ninang, started to sew at home for friends, her reputation spreading by word of mouth. My sister Baby and I grew up with lovely dresses made from remnants of her clients' material. Before that, she sewed for a company exporting ready-made clothes to America.

There is a picture of her with other women in sayas, at their sewing machines, and an American in a white suit, the owner or manager, standing at the door. I remember her picture with five friends in formal wear, taken in a studio. I remember one named, Sixta. I found a letter from Sixta, addressed to Dely, which must have been Fidela's nickname. In back of a photo was a note that they worked in the beading shop of Felicidad Lazaro's relative.

Agrifina/Pinang was an alajera/jeweler. She sold jewels for friends and family who did not wish to be identified: nothing written, just word of honor. I recall her wearing a black terno when she took me with her, all over the city. Wearing a dress instead of a saya, some afternoons she took me to movies, so I saw a lot of Tagalog films which my mother did not think proper for children. I recall only a few scenes— revolucionarios climbing a window; with bolos, running across ricefields. I was mostly interested in the peanuts, fresh corn being roasted in the lobby, sliced singkamas and green mangoes to dip in black bagoong. We brought along copies of *Liwayway* to sit on. There were surot/bedbugs in the chairs.

Tia Pinang often visited relatives. Sometimes walking. Other times, in a calesa. She never took the tranvia which ran along Rizal Avenue, just three streets up from Camarines where we lived. It would have taken her to Santa Cruz, Quiapo, Malate in the heart of Manila south of the Pasig River, where more relatives lived. In a calesa she went to Hulong Duhat, Concepcion and Malabon, the Paez side of the family. Years later, Lola Conching's husband, Lolo Pedro, was found dead, in a banca floating in their fishpond. And still later, their younger son who was mayor was killed when a queso de bola sent to his house exploded. Sometimes, Tia Pinang visited Lolo

Pasio and Lola Dionisa who lived underneath a house on Felix Huertas, fattening a pig to sell on Christmas. Lolo Pasio Cleofas, tall and fair, was born in the Viardo house in San Isidro. He came often for lunch, preferring Fidela's cooking to that of Lola Dionisia who looked like Ima.

Tia Pinang also took me to visit the Viardos in San Bartolome. Tio During lived above his Farmacia, across from the church. I am still in touch with Remy, his youngest daughter. Ate Cording, his oldest daughter, joined us in our Baguio summers at Teachers' Camp. Ate Conchita taught at St. Joseph Academy across their house. With other cousins, Christy Mendoza who lived across us on Araneta and Bella Policarpio, we went on picnics, attended fiestas and Simbang Gabi. The Syjucos, who married into the Viardo family owned a lumberyard. I remember the house, the bathroom as large as a bedroom. The Syjuco cousins were at the wake and funeral of both my parents.

I remember Tia Pinang's friend who lived in an eskinita/callejon in Quiapo. Naty Aquino would look down from the front window and, recognizing us, pull a rope that lifted the door latch. She and Tia Pinang were alajeras/jewellers. Nothing was written, but Tia Pinang remembered the owners and the price they wanted. Going home, my aunt sat carefully in the calesa, the pocket of her saya heavy with gems. Occasionally, working with a licensed realtor, Tia Pinang also sold real estate.

Carmen/Mameng taught in San Isidro. Instructions from the first American teachers were the equivalent of a teacher's diploma so she was certified upon graduating from Grade 6. Tia Mameng's husband, Tomas Ramos, was deputy chief in the Bureau of Internal Revenue. He was killed instantly when his car collided with the car where Lolo Panyong (Epifanio de los Santos/EDSA) was riding. Lolo Panyong was not hurt. Years later, during World War II, Lolo Panyong's son, brought to our house on Araneta Avenue, Lolo Panyong's manuscripts for safekeeping. When Tio Jose returned for them after the War, Fidela discovered that termites had gotten into the boxes stored in the upstairs room. Tia Mameng kept a wreath of black silk flowers in the De Vera house on Elias Street. Ate Luz had married Eusebio de Vera, after he won the Sweepstakes riding Semiramis. Tia Mameng later became an Iglesia ni Cristo. I watched her being baptized, in a basement pool. Lolo Pasio's wife was an Iglesia and must have converted Tia Mameng. Relatives of Tio Tomas lived in San Jose, near a dam. I remember his sisters. Tia Monang was in my short story, "Triptych for a Ruined Altar."

Catalina started teaching fourth grade upon graduation from the Philippine Normal School with Tia Nitang, Lola Kikay's second daughter. A model teacher, Taling was soon assigned to the Department of Education, Curriculum Division. She also wrote textbooks for Macaraig Publishers, and for Ginn & Company of Boston, whose Manila office was near Luneta. While the company officials conferred with Mom, I chose books to take home. Mr. George Miller said, I could take as many as I liked. He also gave me Golden Shower seeds. In the *Friends of the Flower World* which my mother wrote, there might be a picture of me, and a Golden Shower. Unfortunately, we have no copies of the book. Ginn & Company editors treated Mom to dinner when she visited Boston. My short poem "The Ant" was published by the *Philippine Journal of Education* for which my mother wrote. I remember receiving a check for one peso, and hiding it in the escribana under the santols.

In the mornings, either Miss. Herminia Ancheta, or Miss. Trinidad Sion, passed by my mother in a calesa. The Bureau of Education was near the Zoo, the Mehan Garden and the new Opera House; not far from the Philippine Normal School. I remember a picture there: long tables set for hundreds, women teachers wearing sayas, the men suits; and I, seated between my mother and my father at one table.

MY PARENTS

My father, Francisco Figueroa Ty, was born in Calbiga, Samar to Jose Ty and Tarcila Gaborne Figueroa. His father died when Francisco was young and Lola Silay moved to Masbate with her daughter Nena and her husband David Muro. I was close to their oldest daughter Rosario, who attended Far Eastern University before World War II. My father's high school grades earned him the Samar Congressman's recommendation to the Philippine Military Academy in Baguio where he topped the entrance test.

In the Summer Capital, he met my mother who summered in Baguio with the family of Lolo Jose Paez, general manager of the Manila Railroad. Tia Nena Paez Lozano recalled my father coming to their Railroad Cottage on a mola; "so dashing in his uniform." There was an album of my father's years in the PMA, but anay had feasted on it, as on Lolo Panyong's papers. I found only one photo of Dad in his PMA uniform. Years later, Len and I stopped by Bookmark which had just published *The Peninsulars*. Tia Ging Vibar, one of Lolo Jose's daughters, told us Lolo Jose was sick, so we visited him in Malate; and Len met Lolo Jose. Lola Merced had passed on by then. When Tia Pinang took me visiting, before the War, I watched Lola Merced eating atis with a spoon. She was beautiful. On Christmas, she let me pick my gift from their tree, as big as those in the department stores.

Later, my father decided to become an engineer and resigned from the PMA to enroll at the Mapua Institute of Technology, topping the entrance test there, as well. Lolo Jose, general manager of the Manila Railroad, hired him upon his graduation. Impressed by the appointment, his cousin, Jose Costelo, wrote him a long letter from Los Angeles, starting a long correspondence about growing up in Calbiga: the escapades that drew them back to Samar on vacations.

In 1930, my parents married, after which they lived with Nanay and the family in Camarines. I was born at Mary Chiles Hospital. My mother continued working at the Bureau of Education, later also teaching at the National University; my father was line engineer in the Manila Railroad, assigned to extend the lines from Tutuban, the main station. Right away, they started saving for a house which my father designed, with windows all around. Those along the stairs were the full height of the house. He planned on narra floors upstairs and marble tiles below. When they had enough to put down on a lot, they chose Northern Hills behind the monument to Andres Bonifacio, buying 1,000 square meters with their saved salaries and my mother's royalties.

On Fridays when my father came home for the weekend, my mother walked Baby and me to meet him at the Blumentritt station: our hair braided, face powdered, wearing dresses that Fidela sewed from remnants of her customers' material. Weekends, my father took us to Quiapo, where he

15

lifted me up behind the altar so I could kiss the Nazareno's foot. Other times he took Baby and me to the photographer. With his Kodak Brownie, he also took our pictures at Luneta, against the Jockey Club fence; at the Tiwi Hot Springs in Bicol, and other places where we vacationed. One time my father brought home a parrot. It repeated whatever it heard spoken. My father had more fun with it than we.

Dad retired with the reputation that he continued to live in the same house, of not using Railroad Stocks to improve his house. He also refused to disclose to anyone where the new lines were being built; did not make use of the information to enrich himself. At Tutuban, where his office was, he often had lunch in the carinderias instead of in restaurants, paying for the passengers he guessed could use the amount to buy pasalubong. One time an old woman looked for him in order to thank and bless him. When the house needed repairs, he hired Railroad workers and paid them extra. Tia Fidela gave them lunch. Dad remembered all those in Calbiga who were kind to him when he was growing up. On his death bed, he asked me to look for the children of those benefactors so he could return the kindness.

My mother never left the Bureau of Education despite several good offers. One was from Ginn & Company regarding textbook publication. On a Triangular Fellowship from the UN, she worked on the Bill of Rights for children. She retired as Chief of the Elementary School Curriculum Division, in the Bureau of Education, after years of attending conferences in South East Asia as well as giving workshops in the Philippines, as far north as Bangued, Abra. She spoke without notes and many marveled at her wide expertise. The work took a toll on

16

her health. Twice, that I know of, a taxi driver brought her home when she lost consciousness at the Dangwa bus station. I pray for those strangers, who out of the sheer goodness of their hearts, brought her home. And for the jeep drivers who similarly brought Tia Pinang home when she was injured on her way from her store in Dasmariñas. Unexpected and random acts of kindness. After Mom retired from the Bureau, she worked in UP, on a population study, INNOTECH. By then she had the use of a car.

Lola Silay, Tio David and Tia Nena visited us in Camarines whenever there were religious festivals in Manila. Sundays, Lola Silay would attend three to four Masses inside Intramuros. They came for the Eucharistic Congress in 1936. Lola Silay had a comfortable childhood and married life. Lolo Jose's lucrative abaca business allowed her to indulge in her love of jewelry. After he died, she supported the family by selling the jewels, one at a time, also by making ampao/pinato. She had several sisters and a brother who was a priest.

In Ninang Fidela's aparador were the clown costumes she sewed for my parents to wear at the annual Carnivals in Manila. Mom had tiaras to go with her gowns. The stones were rhinestones. Not knowing this, a burglar took them, leaving the contents of the aparador scattered on the floor; photographs among the clothes.

Just before WWII started, my father took us—my mother, Ate Remy and me—to Calbiga. I remember myself in a line of relatives waiting to kiss the hand of the lola being waked. I remember the old church and cemetery, the river and bamboos growing along the banks. After the War was over, I remember my father coming home crying, having found out from a relative that his mother, Lola Silay, had died, along with his sister Nena/Blandina, in the hills; hiding from the Japanese. Tio Peping Castelo held on to the hope their graves would be found and they could be buried in Calbiga but Tio David could not find the mango tree he had marked with a cross over their names. When we returned, we found out Lolo Pasio had died.

Relatives often came to Camarines. From San Isidro Tio Gorio Trinidad, husband of Tia Paca, Lola Kikay's oldest daughter, brought sacks of special rice: fine binuhangin, fruity elon-elon grown only for family. Others brought atis, mango, suha, vegetables. Tio Edong Aquino came from Tarlac. One time, his youngest daughter Corazon/Aton came to visit, riding the train with my father. Relatives from Malabon brought patis, bagoong, bangus, fresh and smoked. Then chairs were brought out to the sidewalk where neighbors and friends joined the family feast under the seresa tree, enjoying Fidela's San Isidro potahes. She served nilaga, fresh lumpia, adobo, pochero, arroz valenciana if just meats, paella if with seafood. Guests agreed her meals were better than those from cookbooks or restaurants. Mr. Fox, a neighbor who worked in the US Commissary in the Port Area, gave her heavy pans, coming over with Aling Imang and the two girls, my age.

Under the seresa my aunts grew gumamela, rosal, azucena which passersby admired from the sidewalk. From the eaves, covering the upstairs window, Tia Fidela hang pots of orchids Dad brought from Bicol. These were watered early so that drippings would not fall on those walking to work below. In the back, past the kitchen, there were more plants, among clay jars of fish, the colors as bright as flowers. I recall, cupping the fish in my hand to flush down the toilet so they could find their way to the sea. Shards of glass topped the dividing wall. Lines of laundry shifted the sunlight.

GEORGE WASHINGTON ELEMENTARY SCHOOL

A t five I started first grade, saling pusa until I was old enough to be officially enrolled, so my mother was surprised when I was accelerated to second grade. Preciosa Cruz, daughter of the principal was a classmate. So were the Olmedo sisters who invited me to their birthdays—I remember the balloons; also, Purificacion Parenas who attended my parents' wake at Loyola in 1982 and 1990. I kept class pictures of trips to museums, to the aquarium in the walls of Intramuros. My Grade 3 teacher was Mrs. Giron. Grade 4 was Mrs. Marcela Garcia who accelerated me to Grade 5. I became friends with her daughters Erlinda and Mona. Mona spent her first American Christmas with Len and me in Watertown. Gretchen was newly born then.

Pinang walked Baby and me to and from George Washington School in a black dress, not a saya which was for visiting family and friends. Leaving Camarines, we turned left at Ima's store, went down Felix Huertas, turned left, then right, past Mrs. Butte's large house. Across from the main gate, during recess, pupils could cross to stores selling sliced green mangoes, turnips. I was not supposed to buy those but classmates offered me bites, smeared with heko, a dark bagoong. My one centavo was for the pan de sal filled with sautéed salmon sold at Home Economics.

Mondays we had opening ceremonies in the Dimasalang corner of the front yard. Large trees shaded the side streets. Independence Day was observed with flags, the Philippine flag below the American. Older students wore costumes representing heroes. Uncle Sam's suit could have been sewn from an American flag. On other holidays, pupils wore costumes appropriate to the celebration.

At the end of the day, teachers walked out of the gate, the women and men separately, until they crossed into Dimasalang. We played in the yard until Tia Pinang came for us. Then we walked back to Camarines.

THE WAR

When the Japanese bombed Manila, December 8, 1941, we sheltered in the Manila Jockey Club at the end of Camarines. The concrete building quickly filled with neighbors, their family and friends, but being just outside the main gate, we got first rights to the space under the main stairs where relatives from San Isidro joined us. Along with beddings, we carried with us, pots and pans, dishes.

Everyone believed the War would last just a few weeks after Pearl Harbor was bombed December 7, Sunday, which was Monday December 8, Immaculate Conception in the Philippines. But the Japanese attack continued. Fires spread over the city, darkening the sky with thick smoke. Dogfights suddenly crisscrossed the sky. We cheered the few planes without a red sun on the tail. Sadly outnumbered, the Philippine planes led by Captain Jesus Villamor, were still able to shoot down several enemy planes. Luz Villamor, niece of the pilot, was a classmate at UP Law, 1949-1955.

For a time, Philippine Army soldiers on their way to Bataan stopped to quarter at the Jockey Club. That Christmas, waiting for a boat back to Masbate, Ate Rosario Muro made little gift bags—toothpaste, candies, shoelaces, cards—to give the soldiers on their way to Bataan. The news from Bataan and, then, Corregidor were not heartening. Many died in the Death March when Japanese soldiers randomly bayoneted the soldiers; and beheaded officers.

The Japanese entered Manila after New Year, three weeks after it attacked Pearl Harbor and Manila. I recall Tia Pinang and me walking along Taft on our way to Lolo Jose when a Japanese officer on a mola started down the middle of Taft directly towards us. Tia Pinang whispered, "We'll keep walking. Do not look at him."

With Manila occupied, the Japanese commandeered the Jockey Club. Sentries appeared in the streets. We kept our windows closed but heard about people being shot or bayoneted if they did not bow low enough to please the sentries. One day, after Bataan had fallen, Tio Piling, second son of Lolo Pasio suddenly appeared at our door with a bullet in his chin. A Japanese officer had shot him in the face during the Death March. We could not bring Tio Piling to a doctor. Lolo Jose Albert was too far away to call, and it was not safe to walk in the streets. Years after the War ended, the bullet was still lodged in Tio Piling's jaw. I can still see it, as I recall the harrowing stories about the Death March Tio Piling narrated. The Japanese shot civilians who tried to give the soldiers water and food, shot soldiers who fell, too weakened to walk on to the concentration camp in Capas. Japanese officers in trucks, swung their sabers at the line of American prisoners, beheading them as they walked below.

Relatives stopped coming to Camarines. It was no longer safe to travel even in the city. When we received underground newspapers, Tia Fidela immediately sewed them inside pillows. The year World War II begun, a few months after, we moved from Camarines into the house my father had designed and built in Northern Hills. It faced west, so we saw the sun setting over the golf course next to University Avenue where the Onrubias and Violas lived; and later, the Villanuevas who bought the Churchill house where, during the war and shortly after, we held meetings with friends in the neighborhood. It was the only property with pine trees along the fence. Beyond was Caloocan, Malabon and Manila Bay.

From the back of our house, we could see the Bonifacio Monument Guillermo Tolentino designed. There were just one or two houses on each hectare block, with rice fields between. Japanese trucks constantly plied Rizal Avenue Extension, four blocks east of us.

We were now too far into the country for relatives and friends to visit. I recall only once that Nanay's cousin walked to our house from Malabon. She was dressed simply though she owned a lumberyard and other businesses, and lived in a large house. She brought Nanay fruits, and did not stay long. From the stories they exchanged, I got a sense of the larger family I had not met, from whom we were separated by the Japanese Occupation.

During the War, I was mostly alone with Nanay who recounted stories of the Revolution against Spain, of the War with the Americans during the past century, early into the next. Always, she ended her stories with, "Someone should write about this." We had books from Dr. George Miller of Ginn & Company, which filled several shelves in the library my father built next to the stairs, but these were grade school textbooks.

We had nothing about the Revolution against Spain and War with the Americans.

We began a different life. In the yard, Tia Fidela started planting upo, gourds and sweet potatoes, beans; and flowers. Tia Pinang and I walked to Gulod to buy a tree and have it cut for firewood. While waiting, we ate on the floor of the farmer's hut, sharing their meal. Years later I learned that the farmer lost the land where his family had lived for generations, when a rich family who owned a university, registered the title in their name, knowing Impong Sepa and her husband had been unaware of the legal requirement. My short story, "Dead Well" is about such duplicitous acquisitions by the rich in the Philippines. On her way to market in Caloocan, Impong Sepa would stop by the house to talk with Nanay, bring her vegetables; and have a cup of coffee with her. Ninang had been given large red beans. Roasted and ground, they tasted like coffee, so she served the brew during the War, and shared the seeds. People said it tasted like real coffee. I found a photo of Impong Sepa against the trellis by the tall window along the stairs.

My father planted saplings of duhat, atis, caimito, seresa, chico, mango which was as fine as peaches. Weekends Dad worked in the backyard, trimming branches. When typhoons blew down the large duhat, he rented a crane to pull it back in place. The large zapote in front shaded the front porch, but never bore fruit.

In the flowerboxes below the downstairs windows, Ninang planted chrysanthemums. One day, Japanese soldiers forced the gate open and cut as many of the stems as they could, shouting and laughing. They were just as loud as those in the Quintos house, who took their bath in the front yard, wearing almost nothing. Another time, at night, soldiers came with a Japanese civilian who ordered us to leave immediately. My mother remembered a Colonel Shimazu had just come to the house asking her to open a school for neighborhood children, offering desks and books in the Japanese language. The civilian kept shouting until my mother mentioned the Colonel's plan. The next week, desks arrived at the house. We were lucky. Many neighbors were immediately thrown out on the street.

One day, Japanese soldiers from Malabon came, house to house, looking for guerrillas. Those arrested—pointed out by a man with a bayong over his head—were seen hanging from trees in the churchyard and at the elementary school near the Monument. My father came out and quietly told the interpreter, "This is Caloocan. Caloocan starts at this fence." The Japanese took my father's word. Weeks later, another group of Japanese soldiers came from the Caloocan. My father told them, "This is Malabon. The boundary is that fence," pointing to the other fence. The Japanese took him at his word.

Widespread scarcity resulted after the Japanese began sending food to Japan. People were dying in the streets of Manila, bloated from having only coconut to eat. Market stalls were empty. Tia Pinang and I walked to Malabon to buy dried fish, the size of fingerlings. People were lucky to find binlid, the cracked grains that used to be fed only to chickens. One time a man knocked at the gate. He had not eaten for days. Ninang served him the rice she was saving for breakfast, with adobo sauce left in the pot from supper. Late one night my father arrived from Bicol with bigas in the legs of his trousers. He and his crew had found a cavan in an abandoned enemy truck. Dad devised a way for them to bring the rice home:

taking off their trousers, they tied the ends, filled the legs with rice and carried the pants across their shoulders. Like the taho vendor with his pails.

Four more years waiting for the Americans to return, as General Douglas MacArthur had promised. Ninang's hopes were lifted each time she saw the V sign in the house and in the yard. It could be a shadow, a strip of light. Meanwhile, trucks kept bringing American soldiers to the Japanese camp at the end of Araneta. If we happened to be in the porch, we waved to the Americans. This scared Ninang Fidela who was afraid the Japanese would shoot us.

The house behind us was occupied by Japanese pilots. We watched them being trucked out in the morning. At night we waited to see how many returned; usually less. We had a sense they were bombing the Visayas for we heard Americans had landed in Leyte. One night, the Japanese houseboy suddenly appeared at the kitchen window, while we were having lugao and dilis. He had climbed the wall between the houses, to bring a whole fish on a platter, cooked like tocho; and stayed to watch us eat. Days later, he cut out part of the wall, so he could just walk into our yard. Sometimes he brought candies, like tiny boiled eggs with a yellow center. We figured these were the rations of the pilots who did not return. One day, we realized the pilots' house was empty. It was quiet and dark. We saw Japanese soldiers crouched outside, but they disappeared before we could run from the house.

A few days later, Mr. Quintos and other neighbors came to tell my father American soldiers were seen near BBB, the brewery in Balintawak, so my father went with them to meet the Americans on their way to Manila having, we found out, landed in Subic. At the Bonifacio Monument people cheered the soldiers heading to liberate the Americans concentrated at the Santo Tomas University. Mr. George Miller had been imprisoned there but my mother had been unable to send him supplies through Felix; and we did not know where he now was.

The guerrillas and American soldiers approaching from south finally joined those from the north at the Pasig River. Manila was liberated, but it was destroyed; second only to Warsaw in the devastation. Newspapers showed piles of the dead; buildings and churches in ruins. Gutted, Manila looked like a dead city.

A contingent of the American army camped across our house in Northern Hills, occupying several blocks. My father's dog would get into the camp, bring back partly opened cans of tinned meat. On pay day, the soldiers gathered outside the downstairs windows which opened outward, each section as wide as a bank teller's window. After the soldiers had all received their pay, the paymasters left the house, leaving candies for us and the families who had asked to stay in the backyard until they could continue their way back home. The soldiers who walked with rifles around the house were last to leave.

The War still was not over for us. Tia Mameng, Ate Luz and her son Dick were still somewhere in Manila taking care of Tia Nene's store after the Policarpio family evacuated to San Jose. After days of seeing Manila burning, my father and Ninang Fidela decided to bring them home. Walking, they met people coming out of the city with stories of Japanese shooting civilians. Tia Mameng thought it was her obligation to remain in the store, so my father and Ninang had to return without them. Instead of taking the streets where Japanese soldiers marched, they went in and out of houses, finally reached the North Cemetery where they walked between graves toward the Monument. It took them two days.

Weeks later, Tia Mameng, Ate Luz and year-old Dick, finally arrived. Running, hiding among the dead in the streets, they reached the Pasig River where guerrillas and American soldiers were helping people across. They were covered with blood from dropping down among the dead in the streets whenever Japanese soldiers approached. They told of Japanese soldiers shooting the priests and nuns in the colleges in Manila, smashing infants against the walls of the Philippine General Hospital, of soldiers entering houses and shooting everyone as they came out.

CALOOCAN HIGH SCHOOL

With World War II over—schools started. I was in Mrs. Lutgarda Bascon's Grade 6 class when War began, so though I did not go to school during the War, I was ready for high school when classes resumed. I passed the high school entrance test. After being briefly at the Cecilio Apostol Elementary School near the Bonifacio Monument, Caloocan High took over the Manila Railroad cottages along Samson Road. The British General Manager's former cottage was large enough for several classrooms. Large acacias shaded the yard. We walked under their shade to classes in the other cottages.

We went to daily Mass at San Roque Church beside the High School. When a classmate was waked there, we joined the family vigil until her burial. The deep well in the back porch of the rectory, the overhang of trees gave the feeling of the years past. Nanay's church in San Isidro was also San Roque.

From Araneta, Baby and I walked to school on El Heroes del 96, which the Revolucionarios used some fifty years before. In Mr. Arsenio Manuel's history class at UP, I learned that General Antonio Luna waited, in the General Manager's cottage, for the Americans to come by train, chasing Aguinaldo to Malolos. The fact made more real Nanay's stories about the Philippine-American War.

Neneng Nebrida, Bartolome and Florentino Silayan were in the first group. During Liberation, the Nebridas ran down Mango Street to shelter in our house when bombers flew overhead. Other neighbors, Marita Ramos, Mike Viola, whose grandfather supported Jose Rizal when he lived in Europe, enrolled in private colleges in Manila. In school, Norma and Sonia Gandionco, Fe Del Rosario and I formed the Little Women. I was supposed to be Jo; Fe, Beth; Norma, Meg; and Sonia, Amy. The Berg sisters were in our class. The family had moved to Northern Hills from Manila, during the war, to escape being sent to the Japanese concentration camp for foreigners. Mercy and I were in the Dutch Wooden Clogs folk dance. One Independence Day parade on Luneta, Mercy was on a float.

Joining Our Lady of Grace's Catholic Youth Organization Norma, Sonia and I were prepared for first confession and first Communion which the War interrupted. We helped register the families starting to settle in Grace Park which was open land before the War. Squatters now filled the area. Fr. Boyd and Fr. Milford were the parish priests. The latter came from Milford, Massachusetts.

Caloocan High had a Girl Scout troop with Dorothy as Scout leader. Mrs. Pelagia Martinez was Scout Master. Her assistant was Miss Evangelina Tolentino, a student of Mom in grade school. We gathered at the Monumento, walked to the farms along the Tuliahan River which Filipino and American soldiers crossed and recrossed, chasing each other during the Philippine-American War. Several miles from where we

31

camped for the day, was the farm of Tandang Sora, where in 1896, the Revolucionarios, having torn their cedulas, waited for the Revolution to start. All the land around felt like sacred ground.

Caloocan High was like family. The homes of classmates and teachers were open for impromptu visits. School parades were cheered from houses lining the main street. We kept in touch for years with Miss Javier, principal; Mrs. Aurora Santos; Miss Naomi Vargas; Miss Perpetua Baello; Miss Pacifica Cordero. Baby and I vacationed with them in Teachers' Camp, Baguio, where we had Santacruzans. The summer I was Reyna Elena, Aling Naty Cruz sewed my saya. Later, she sewed my wedding dress; and after we moved to the States, she sent Gretchen embroidered dresses. A classmate, Elena Sanchez, was the organist when Len and I were wed. Elisa Sanchez, another classmate, also attended.

Whenever I was home, classmates arranged a reunion. The last one I recall was in November, 2002, at the Viajero Restaurant in Quezon City. Elsa Adea, Loida Flores Virina (Vda. de Ben Virina), Augusto Virina, Amy Cruz, Mamerto Banatin, Concordia Dizon, Pepe Paez whose brother Angel was also a classmate, Johnny de la Cruz, Avelina Jose, Manuel Castillo, Adoracion Acuna, Ramon de la Cruz attended. Epitacio Sabandal's son was a priest, assistant chaplain of Southridge School, Alabang. I kept class pictures, as well as my photos wearing the sayas we sewed in Home Economics.

UNIVERSITY OF THE PHILIPPINES
LAW SCHOOL

After Caloocan High, I enrolled at the University of the Philippines with the Gandioncos, but lost touch with Fe del Rosario, until 2020 when Kristian Cordero, editor of Ateneo de Naga University Press, asked Cecilia Brainard, if Belinda Ty in Fe's *Memoir* they were publishing was Linda Ty-Casper. It was too late for Fe and me to meet again. She had passed in 2020, but reading her *Memoir* which her daughters Nathalie and Nina sent me, filled in the lost years. I sent Fe's daughters the wedding card she had sent Len and me in 1956.

Baby and I took the bus taking students from Malabon directly to Diliman. If he saw us coming up Araneta, the driver waited on Samson Road. Going home took longer since we had to take the bus to Quiapo, then a jeepney to Blumentritt, from there a jeep or bus to the Bonifacio Monument, another jeep to Sangandaan which dropped us off at Samson Road to walk two blocks to the house. After we learned to drive and the driver left, Baby and I took the car to UP. My father had a railroad car for his use so he brought my mother to her office on his way to Tutuban. Eventually they got a used car for Mom but Eddie, Ate Luz's son, had to keep it in constant repair. Though they did not splurge on themselves, my parents bought Baby's three sons a new car each.

When UP moved in 1949 to Diliman from Padre Faura in Manila, there were just two buildings. Law and Education faced each other across the Quad—where graduations, the ROTC parades, the Cadena de Amor processions were held. The year I graduated, I gave the speech at the Cadena de Amor procession. The Infirmary was in one of the Quonset huts left by the American army. Faculty housing, student housing took over the other Quonset huts.

In front of the Administration Building stood Guillermo Tolentino's *Oblation*, to symbolize lives dedicated to the country as inspired by Jose Rizal. Classrooms were far apart but there were jeepney routes in the periphery. We mostly walked. One Arbor Day, I joined students planting acacia trees around the campus. I recall Lantern Parades in December, the Carillon tower, Balara and the hills beyond. Red zinnias bloomed all around the campus.

After my Associate Degree, I tried to enroll in the History Department but Professor David Wico suggested Hermy Abejo and I go to the Law School, and return if were rejected. We ended up in the Law School for four years, though we had not intended so. I recall first semester classmates crowding the board where my name topped the honor roll. I was surprised since I had not tried to make the list, did not know one existed. Though I studied hard, I didn't aim to graduate as valedictorian. Everyone in the College was the valedictorian or salutatorian of their high school. I did not take to heart Mrs. Ursula Clemente's advice to plan for the future. What I trusted was Nanay's belief that things will happen if they are supposed to happen. We can only deserve them and be grateful. Mangyayari kung talagang mangyayari. As I recall my life, I realize how right Nanay was. Life can't really be planned or predicted. I never thought I would live abroad, or that writing historical novels would become my life work.

My heart was still set on history, maybe because of Nanay's stories of the Revolution and War with the Americans. One time, Professor Enrique Fernando asked something about interpretation and called my name. Out of the blue, I answered "Context"—the word he wanted. That impressed some, while I tried to figure out how I came up with the word he expected, when my mind was on other things as usual. I remember Professors Ventura in his white suits, Ramon C. Aquino researching in the stacks, Barrios, and Abad Santos, Jose Campos who congratulated me when he read my story, written while preparing for the Bar.

UP Law was a big family. We had known each other since 1949 when we entered Pre-Law. Some were already big names, certain to succeed. I remember Lolita Lavides. Since there were not enough copies of assigned books, she and I took copious notes of those Alex was able to get for the Law Library. We discovered, we did not have to reread our notes, which got coded in our memory in the process of writing.

Classmates exchanged visits. Luz Villamor and her Ate Consoling stayed with Len and me when they came to the States. Len took them to historical sites. I recall, at Faneuil Hall, Luz bought a pair of high heels: to put on just before deplaning in Manila, so as to awe classmates meeting her. Ate Consoling Manguerra Asis was a professor of biology at UP, had written several books. It was in her house I met Mrs. Concepcion

35

Manguerra, Cecilia Brainard's mother who spoke so proudly of Cecilia and her writing.

Louie Mauricio invited us to lunches at the National Press club, bravely reviewed *Dread Empire* during Martial Law for *Panorama*. Buddy Maronilla, also from Malabon, and many others took turns treating the Class to reunions in 5-Star hotels. Flory Orendain sent a lechon to Pansol when Hermy had Nene Abiog, Betty de Jesus Gonzalez and me for the weekend. Class reunions were not annual, but held anytime a classmate came from abroad, or just to get together. Gloria Paculdo took us on a pilgrimage to the Miraculous Virgin of Manaog in Pangasinan. Bart Carale, later Dean of UP Law, invited the class to San Pablo. Len was often fondly included in these reunions.

The Class adopted Gretchen so each time she was home, or taking a year abroad at Ateneo, they included her in Class activities; even arranged for her to interview church and military leaders for her first book, *Fragile Democracies*. Gretchen enjoyed the reunion at Hidden Valley.

Years afterward, classmates joked that I was the class deviate. I had become a writer of historical novels. In the book *50 Years of Women at Harvard*, my rather long letter explained that my training had actually prepared me for such work, my books are briefs for the country, so our history will not be written for us: so we will be part of the world's story, not remain in the footnotes: the world can know and imagine us through our stories.

Do I regret not practicing? Many think I wasted my years of study. Occasionally, I recall trial court at Harvard, where at the end of one session Professor Dershowitz looked at me and said, "You were good. Quite good." Do I regret not taking another year for a doctorate in Jurisprudence as

Professor Brown suggested because of my high grades; or taking a year at Yale after Harvard? Yale extended its scholarship offer another year. But I had to make a choice.

And my UP classmates made up for me in many ways; serving the country as lawyers, law deans, justices and judges, politicians, business entrepreneurs, professors and law book authors, children's book writer and illustrators, newspaper columnist, government officials: a whole gamut of service as attested to by *UP Law '55 Profiles* which Luz Villamor lovingly collected, cajoling everyone until 61 out of 110 finally relented and sent their profiles, including two gravely ill. Whew! And Wow! As Luz exclaimed. Ninoy Aquino was a classmate but few of us recall ever meeting him, only read about his interviewing Luis Taruc, which Gretchen also did for her book, *Fragile Democracies*.

Classmates came from Luzon, the Visayas and Mindanao. Elias Lopez was born "in the hinterland of Davao City" to the Bagobo tribe. Advised by his father to take up law to help the Bagobos, after graduation he ran for City Councilor, starting a life in public service, "slowly and painstakingly setting the pace for Bagobos to enter the modern world." He went on to become Mayor of Davao City, Congressman from the third district of Davao City. He might have become president had he not died young.

Jainal D. Rasul was born in Jolo, Sulu. His dream of becoming a lawyer "was anchored on the desire to help attain for our country the national unity … based on Muslim-Christian reconciliation. The government policy of assimilation … anchored only on Christian principles will inevitably result in religio-cultural genocide for the Muslim minority …. Undoubtedly what is needed is some sort of Federal system … co-participation in government and commonality that will unify our country and people …." His training and expertise in Islamic law and jurisprudence made Jainal a resource and consultant in the Codification of Islamic laws. He has written three books on the subject. He was a member of the Philippine Sharia Institute. As a member of the Supreme Court Committee, Jainal helped draft the Special Rules and Procedure on Sharia Court.

In 1996 when the *Class Profiles* came out, Len and I were invited to speak at the Philippine Centennial Celebration in Manila, so I was able to meet many classmates, even ran into Professor Enrique Fernando during one meeting. UP Law Class '55 looked forward to the 50th year in 2006, but Luz had passed away in 2000. Irreplaceable. Very much missed. The Life of Class '55. The bond. The glue. The *Profiles* she cajoled from classmates is a rare portrait of our country. I dedicated *Fortress in the Plaza* to UP Class '55.

LEN

I n 1953, after the Stanford fellowship, and a year teaching
at Cornell, Len gave up a Fulbright to London and boarded
a cargo boat to Manila. It took him a month to arrive.

Len recalled "the first Filipinos I ever knew were Fel
Sta. Maria and Amador Daguio ... Stanford students in the off-
campus, barracks-style dorm." Especially on long holidays,
when others disappeared home, they were "isolated" together;
Len's folks being 2,000 miles away in Wisconsin. Amador
Daguio wrote about being so homesick, they sang Philippine
Christmas carols in the bus returning them to the dorm, the
driver trying to sing along with them. Len further wrote "what
held us together was our common interest in writing; Fel as a
superior journalist, Amador as a poet regenerate; I as a short
story writer eager to make up for three years spent in the
combat artillery ... For one year we read and advised each
other's work. Then I went to teach at Cornell, tiring of the
academic routine and straight semesters earning a doctorate

and already inclined to accept Fel's invitation to come to UP where I might be useful."

With his doctorate, Len immediately got a teaching position at the University of the Philippines and Ateneo de Manila. He had published in the States—during the Second World War, he sent stories from the European front to the *Southwest Review* whose editors offered to get him a publisher. His dissertation at Madison was on Robert Penn Warren which became the first book on Warren: *The Dark and Bloody Ground* which critics said "paved the way for further study of the Southern writer." For almost 13 years after, Len and Robert Penn Warren corresponded, sharing their academic lives and having to cut the lawn and shovel snow. He invited Len to Connecticut, to New York to see his plays; thanked Len for his comments on his writings. *The Blood Marriage of Earth and Sky* Len's second book on Warren, according to Fred Hobson, is "literary and erudite ... the crowning achievement in the career of an eminent Warren scholar."

Len also lectured in other universities, forging friendships with many writers. His growing reputation led the UP president, Carlos P. Romulo, to write him; expressing his hope that Len would return to the University.

At UP Len boarded with Fel Sta Maria, with whose family he attended the Chapel of the Holy Sacrifice. Len was one of thousands—students, faculty—who walked from Ateneo and UP, accompanying the beloved Fr. John Delany's hearse to the Novitiate and cemetery in Novaliches in 1956.

The first summer, Len also taught at the UP Baguio Extension, rooming with Dick Coller. Len wrote of their nightly cockroach kill in the dorm; six being the maximum catch. Len loved Baguio; loved walking up and down the hills, taking pictures of the sunrise and sunsets from Camp John

Hay, Mansion House, Mines View Park and other heights. One Sunday, he met my father walking up to the Baguio Cathedral for Mass, waited at the bus station to see Dad off to Manila. He loved the weather, the food at Patria Inn, the Igorot carvings in the market where he bought a pipe for his father. We summered at Teachers Camp, and Len often came for Ninang Fidela's San Isidro lunches.

After summer, on the driver's day off, Len drove the car Mom brought back from Stanford to Luneta, for breakfast on the seawall. On Good Friday, he took us to see the flagellantes in Navotas. We went to the fishpond restaurant; to Angat to visit Mr. Magtanggol Santos, Dad's friend, from the Railroad, who brought especially-ordered bibingka which Gretchen remembers. We went to Amaya beach in Cavite, guests of the Abad family. Fr. Cery Abad went on day trips with us when he was at Boston College. There were fiestas and family gatherings in Malabon. We were guests of Virgie Moreno at her Los Indios Bravos where one met other writers. I recall the black lights in the Naughty Room. Among others, we met Ben Cabrera. Sherman Carroll of Readers International used two of his paintings for the covers of *Awaiting Trespass* and *Wings of Stone*.

One time, I recall, I relieved Len at the wheel, and passed some men and a motorcyclist who started to chase us. I drove into the rice fields where the motorcyclist floundered, and we got away safely. Another time I recall, driving on Avenida Rizal when a red sports car passed me so close it nearly hit me, so I overtook it, passed it as close as I could two, three times on the Avenida until the driver sped away.

During the week, Len came to Araneta between his classes; waiting until I came home from the Philippine UNESCO Commission where I worked while waiting to leave for graduate work in the United States. We had several hearings on administrative cases in Malacañang. I worked on a project to help writers get published, on putting together data on Juvenile Delinquency which I planned to study at Harvard. I had been accepted at several universities, Yale offering a "very substantial award"; but we decided on Harvard because Fr. Kunkle/Fr. Grace had offered Len a teaching position at Boston College, a Jesuit University a trolley ride from Cambridge.

I reviewed for the Bar at Padre Faura where I met classmates similarly occupied. Bar results came out February 20. I did not top the Bar. Romy Arguelles asked the *Times* to correct my grade: not 75 but 85. I was 13th by my classmates' count. After the oath taking at the Supreme Court, at the UP Law Luncheon, classmates insisted I get up on the stage.

Len and I had planned our wedding and were waiting for my father to return from Japan where he was on the Manila Railroad Reparations Commission. Waiting for the wedding, I broke open my piggybank. I had $148 dollars. I returned some coins to the piggybank in memory of Nanay who once counted them with me.

Fr. Pacifico, who landed at Leyte with President Sergio Osmeña and General Douglas MacArthur, married us at the Archbishop's Palace, having prepared us at the UP Chapel of the Holy Sacrifice during several meetings. Friends—Hermy, Beatriz, Mona Garcia; Bella gave several showers. Lumen Policarpio, director of UNESCO, scheduled one at The Columbian Club. Tia Pinang had the arras and our rings made at Heacock. Mom and I finally found the lace we wanted. Aling Naty sewed my gown. Ate Luz worked on my trousseau. Her sons Eddie, Jessie and George took care of transportation.

Flowers and decorations were by L. Carlos. Photos by Veluzar. Guests said it was the most organized wedding, ever.

Fel Sta. Maria was best man. Trinidad Sion, my mother's forever friend was Ninang. Dr. Alfredo Morales was Ninong. Baby was Maid of Honor; Hermy Abejo, Beatriz de Jesus and Linda Garcia were sponsors: veil, ring and cord. Elizabeth de Vera was flower girl; Percy Banez was ring bearer. There were the Viardos and Paezes, Policarpios, De Veras, Banezes, Velasquezes, Figueroas, Muros ... Caloocan High classmates, Len's writer friends. Mr. Santos' wife Rina arranged for newspaper coverage of the wedding, including *El Debate*. My father asked only that we hold the reception at D&E, whose owner was also from Samar.

After the wedding, we went up to Baguio where Len and I walked up the hills, under the pine trees. Len took a lot of pictures at the Pines Hotel and along Session Road. Back in Manila, we stayed at Luneta Hotel where we had a direct view of Jose Rizal's Monument. There, friends and family visited, until we left for the States. The night before we left, Len and I looked for Fr. Ortiz and found him in the Quonset hut where he was celebrating Mass for workers and their families. He blessed us for the trip to America.

.

UNITED STATES

A happy airport send-off by family and friends made the trans-Pacific flight less forbidding. We promised to be back soon. They promised to visit us in America. NVM and Narita Gonzalez brought us two natural pearls, which I keep in the original box.

Next: Hong Kong, the Peninsula Hotel and floating restaurant—we took buses to tour the city. Then on to Hawaii to see Len's sister Rose who had married John Silva, whose father came from Lisbon and bought land in Hawaii. The large Silva family welcomed us. John took us around Maui. With the three-year-old twins, John and Joseph, we got up before daybreak to watch sunrise on Mount Haleakala on whose slopes grew a rare plant that grew nowhere else; white flowers arranged on tall stems, like the yucca Len later planted along the Sudbury River. The twins loved books and the library was their favorite place. James Godfrey was born four years later, just before our next visit.

The Republican Convention had taken over San Francisco, so after seeing the sights, we took the train to Boston, passing through the Midwest. From the train we saw mountain ranges, the endless plains, the edge of cities. The landscape was too vast to contain in photographs. Before dropping off at Nebraska, a woman wished us well, hoped our expectations were not dashed in America. Did she intuit my father's fear I would face discrimination in America?

His fears were proved right. I remember in a trolley, in Cambridge, a woman stared at me and said, "Go back where you came from." Briefly taken aback, I told her to do the same, and remained across from her, until she looked away. She was quiet until she dropped off before Rice Street, my stop. Another time in Filene's Basement, a woman pushed towards me the rack of clothes I was checking. Without hesitating, I pushed the clothes back towards her. She walked away. A third time, a black woman stared at me, looking me over in a superior manner. I stared back at her, and looked her up and down, until she moved away. But those were mild forms, compared to current Asian hate which includes being punched in the face, shoved into the street, being stabbed or shot. I might not know how to respond to that.

There was time only for a short stop at Fond du Lac, Wisconsin before heading East to Boston. In the midst of the first family gathering, Len's father, Louis Casper disappeared, returning with a box of chocolates for me. Besides Louis and Caroline Eder, there were Louis and Mary, Ruth and Ed Shank, Leo and Germaine, Rita and Joe Willman, and Roma. Larry and Ginny were in Tennessee. All the sons had served in World War II, as did his sister Rita who was an army nurse. Larry brought home medals, including a Purple Heart. So did Joseph

Willman. Len did not get wounded so he received two bronze stars. The war had been over some ten years.

Len's family gave us wedding presents, dishes and linen to start us off in Cambridge. In Boston we discovered that the apartment Josefina Constantino had reserved for us had been rented out. Len found a small one, on Rice Street. On the Mass Avenue end was an Irish pub; at the other, Our Lady of Pity, a French church. Len understood the sermons because his mother Caroline was from Alsace-Lorraine, spoke French and German.

After Mass on Sundays, we went across to the bakery. Next door was the laundromat where Len brought our wash after teaching at Boston College in Chestnut Hill, an hour away. For me, Harvard was just 15 minutes by trolley. I could walk home, as Len and I did when he passed by me after school, stopping at furniture stores on Mass Avenue. That way, we saved two quarters each way. Harvard Square had movie houses, banks, a Wursthaus, specialty stores like Olsen's where cards were sold singly instead of in boxes, lovely gift items, small jewelry. And in front of the trolley station, the Out of Town newspaper stand whose owner saved the Sunday *New York Times* for us to pick up on Monday, saving us a trolley ride.

At Boston College, Len met other University of Wisconsin graduates: Al Duhamel, Ed Nehls, Dick Hughes. The rest of the faculty were from Harvard, Columbia, and local universities. Mostly Irish, a few Italians. Len was the only one of German/French descent. There was nevertheless, a pervading sense of family. We invited students and faculty to the house, were in turn invited by the other faculty.

46

During Christmas, the Jesuits feted faculty children at the College celebrations. There were special nights at the Museum of Fine Arts.

Everyone wore a suit. Every classroom had a crucifix. Classes started and ended with a prayer.

But the early years were heaven. Len's creative writing students won several prizes at the annual *Atlantic Monthly* Collegiate Creative Writing Contests. Overall, 31 novels were written by his students in Creative Writing. Len was voted The Heights Teacher of the Year in 1962. Aside from teaching, he also wrote, now mostly critical books and essays in American Literature, as well as in Philippine Literature for encyclopedias, journals. He was contributing editor for *Panorama, Literature East and West, Solidarity, Filipinas* and many other journals; a member of MLA panels in the US and in the Philippines. Len was appointed to major BC committees: Academic Council, University Promotions Committee, Faculty Caucus, Dean Search Committee, Executive Committee, Mellon Grant Committee, Search Committee for Honorary degrees, and others. Off-campus, he was consultant for the Rockefeller Foundation, the Asia Society; was trustee of St. Paul House of Studies. One Boston College president asked him to be Chair of the English department; another, to be Dean of Arts and Science. Len explained that he was a teacher, not an administrator.

Fr. John Leonard, who landed with American troops in Subic, wrote two books about World War II in the Philippines; inscribed copies for Len. Richard Cardinal Cushing signed Len's copy of *The World's Cardinal*: With affection and blessings and gratitude for the important part you played in the publication of this book.

At conferences held in Boston and Cambridge Len reconnected with other University of Wisconsin graduates. Charles Hoffmann and Tess lived on Little Rest Road, site of King Philip's Indian War encounters in Rhode Island. Gretchen remembers Tess knitting her a sweater, carrying her through her garden. Charles was the brother of Frederick Hoffmann who mentored Len at Madison, and who invited Len to join him each time he moved to a different teaching position. Len loved Boston College and made excuses. Len also met again, Tom Gullason then at the University of Rhode Island. Tom showed us the Boston he knew growing up. Exchanging visits, we explored Rhode Island's beaches and parks: among them Arcadia, Burlington. At Champlin in Point Judith, we got lobster pots to cook in the sand at Moonstone Beach. We visited Tom's parents in Watertown.

The summer Len taught a writing course at URI, we stayed with Gladys Simmons on Ministerial Road, summering with her each year after. She had lived in West Alys, Wisconsin. When her husband passed away, she returned to build a house on her father's extensive farms, and offered Len two acres across from Larkin Pond on which to build but the commute would have been long. Nevertheless, for almost 20 years we summered with her. She doted on Gretchen, offered us her collection of cut glass, but we had no room, so I accepted one for Gretchen. Once, we were able to convince her to go back with us and she enjoyed the visit, but missed her dog, Pal. Gretchen loved Pal.

WATERTOWN

The last year at Harvard we moved from Cambridge to Watertown, on Carver Road. The apartment was larger and we could invite more friends to dinner. I had learned more complicated dishes. My mother visited when she got grants to the Radcliffe Publishing Seminar, to the UNESCO. Tia Nene Policarpio and Ate Mameng stayed with us. And UP friends, enrolled at Harvard or Radcliffe: Ching Dadufalza, Nieves and SV Espistola, my former Philosophy professor, Ruben Cuyugan and his family, among others, came to visit. Len took them around the city and historical sites.

Lottie Johnson, our landlady, often was at the door before 6 a.m. with a plate of freshly made doughnuts. She and her sister Martha invited us for salmon dinners on the Fourth of July. Lottie's husband had built their two-story house, designed the wallpapers. It was only after his death that she discovered he owned rental properties on Atlantic Avenue where he had a haberdashery. She was from St. John, Canada and Len took her to the train station when she went home to visit. One time to donate an organ to her church.

We lived across from Belmont and attended the Lady of Mercy church. On Rosary Hill, across from church there were fireworks on the Fourth. Gretchen was born in St. Elizabeth's Hospital, Boston. Ruth McAleer gave us her doctor's name, Charles Sullivan who delivered both Gretchen and Tina, 12 years apart; and also Kathleen Lynch Moncata, the elder care lawyer we met at the Senior Center in Framingham, 2015. I remember Mary, Charlie's nurse.

When I had to return to St. Elizabeth after Gretchen was born, Len would bring her, in her bassinet, to Ed Hirsh, the English chair, until class was over. He and Margaret, and their children, loved to have Gretchen.

One more time Gretchen went to St. Elizabeth. She was brushing her teeth when she suddenly leaned against my face. I had never seen anyone lose consciousness but I knew to call for help. The police came right away and took us to St. Elizabeth. Len came from school to find Gretchen had recovered but was being kept for observation. The next morning, Len and I went to pick up Gretchen. She was not in her room but was being carried up and down the hall by a young doctor who said, as Ruth McAleer often remarked, that Gretchen was the perfect Ivory Soap baby. He reluctantly let us take Gretchen home.

Gretchen was baptized at Our Lady of Mercy. She and I would walk, from church to Cushing Square for ice cream; meeting with neighbor children and their mothers. Lotte often urged us to go hear Norman Vincent Peale, so she could babysit Gretchen. When after about three years, we decided to buy a house, Lotte tried to make us stay. When there was a delay in our moving to Framingham, she insisted we stay with her meantime. She liked the house we bought. The Sudbury River, in back, reminded her of St. John in Canada.

FRAMINGHAM

We were lucky to find Waino and Doris Peterson's house. The day the realtor Mr. Mulle took us to see it, he had shown us houses in Wayland, Lexington and other area towns, but the houses were either too close to a main street, or beyond our budget. The Peterson house appeared to have been waiting for us. Marigolds grew along both sides of a white fence. Newly planted trees, a circle of white birches, framed the Sudbury River in the back.

Immediately, we had family on Simpson Drive. Across were Ralph and Dorie Johnson, and Bob and Kay Monahan. On our side of Simpson Drive, to our right was Silvestre and Josephine Mangini who had paid cash for their house and told us stories of Framingham, to which they had moved from Italy. Next to the Manginis were the Flemings. Sue and I both gardened. Gretchen played with Missy and Kathy Fleming, and with Colleen Monahan; walked with them to Brook Water School, to CCD at St. Jeremiah.

In the winter, each family along the Sudbury River, cleared the snow behind their property; helped extend each other's skating area. Gretchen and Tina learned to skate from other children on Simpson Drive. In the winter when the ice was over 12 inches thick, the Reiter boys—Tom, Greg and Edmund--would come over to skate. Bob and Jo Reiter were part of the Boston College family. Marge Fitzgerald would bring complete dinners. She and John often invited the department for dinners, and pool parties. Their parties were excellent.

St. Jeremiah was two streets up from Simpson Drive. The Daily Mass Group went to each other's house for coffee after Mass, exchanged plants, helped with the committees, took parishioners to medical appointment or shopping. Once friends surprised me with coffee in the Rectory since I was going to the Philippines. Irene Colonna baked a cake and topped it with a frosted version of the Philippine flag. Fr. Dan Quinn baptized Tina just before heading out to the horse races. Without being asked Fathers James Hession, John Morris, Joseph Flynn said Masses for my parents when they were ill. Phyllis Nicoli, the secretary, xeroxed my interviews in the local paper, even tacked them onto the board. Fr. Flynn said my prose was "felicitous." One of Len's first students at Boston College, Fr. Walter Edyvaen sent them copies of "Fellow Passengers" which Fr. John Farrell had seminarians at St. John, read during Lent.

Sundays, Mr. and Mrs. Jane and Jake Stirml would ask to hold Tina while we received Communion. Years later, I found letters from Len's sister Roma mentioning the name Stirmls in the Casper family tree. I found too late the letters Len kept tightly folded in a box. Also on the Casper family tree was the name Hatch/Hatches. The second husband of Emy

Arcellana's mother was a Mr. Hatch. I had no idea when I met him that his name was also in Len's family tree.

Sr. Mary Helen Glennon slept over when it was too late to drive back to the Sisters of St. Joseph's House in Arlington. When she found out I had not been to the Holy Cross Cathedral in Boston, she insisted on taking me to attend an ordination there. Though people tried to dissuade her because parking would be tight, when we arrived there was space by the front door. Fr. O'Connor delayed the annual picnic at his family's house in Marshfield until I returned from the Philippines. Fr. Michael Fillie from Sierra Leone, often asked to be taken for lunch at the Harvard Faculty Club. I took along as many as could fit in the car: Ceil Wohler, Dot McLaughlin and Grace Corrigan.

When the closing of church buildings resulted from the clergy sexual abuse, we were part of the vigil to keep St. Jeremiah open for a few more years. Michael and Delina Sannicandro, Ann and Jim Capobianco, Wayne Larkin, Mary Beth Carmody, Louise and Peter Ditammi, John and Phyllis Olszewski, Ceil Wohler, Irene Seekings, Veronica Switlekowski, and more than half the parishioners took turns, night and day, staying in the church to keep it open. Len took his own vigil schedule. We wrote to the Cardinal, who refused to meet with parishioners from parishes he closed even after Len reminded him that Jesus went out to bring back a single lost sheep. No replies. Finally, the Cardinal sold the St. Jeremiah for two million, having also taken the church funds, to pay for the clergy sexual abuse cases.

On Holy Days Len and I invited to dinner parishioners without families. I had learned to make crown roast, relleno, paella; to poach salmon. Dessert might be lace wafers, leche flan or Le Succès/Sans Rival—using the French Chef's recipe, but making 14 instead of 7 layers. Gretchen says it's her favorite dessert. She and I watched Julia Child's programs. At Julia's last East Coast appearance in Wayland, I mentioned this and Julia beamed as she signed the book for Gretchen. Tina helped served mercy meals at the house for parishioners left alone after a death in the family.

I joined Birthright, Nuclear Freeze, Pro-Life, Prison Ministry. Jeanne Prifti and I attended classes on religion at the Lady Help of Christian Church where we met Mother Teresa. I taught CCD, and years later, so did Tina. CCD met at the teacher's house. I made a point of having snacks, time to play in the backyard, rewards for knowing the lessons. Sometimes Len took over. After Grade 8, I had to give up teaching and the children who had been with me those years said, "There goes our CCD." I almost changed my mind. But I was in too many committees in church, several writing groups; and arthritis was starting in my joints. And I had those books to write. But I was always happily surprised when one of the children asked Tina about me, as I had been glad to know some mothers still asked Sr. Mary Helen if their children could be assigned to my class.

There was no lack of activities in the Boston area. We became part of the Iskwelahang Pilipino. Len enjoyed the annual Lowell Food Festival where he helped serve the pancit, adobo, fried lumpia, turron and other Filipino specialties. Lines appeared longest at the Filipino table. Friends watched incredulously as Len ate dinuguan. Dr. Lucy Lee/Aunt Lucy said, "Len is the only American who eats dinuguan." I learned later that the Germans have a similar dish which Len's mother had served the family. Sundays, Iskwelahang directed by Cris Castro, offered classes: language, culture, songs, dance, art. Venue was local churches, or the Perkins School for the Blind.

One Santacruzan, Tina was Reyna Elena. Luisa Garcia took her picture with Mama Garcia, Julie Ott, Eddie Endriga and Len. Cris lent Tina a beautiful blue saya. Luisa taught me how to transition from the typewriter to the computer, brought me a computer when I hesitated.

There was Lourdes Javier's Filipino Association of Greater Boston. Restoring Sight Foundation to prevent and treat blindness in the world and in the Philippines was under Drs. Felipe Tolentino and Roland Houle. Its many supporters included two Spanish counts: Marques de Elzaburu and Marques De Commillas who funded it generously. For years Dr. Tolentino had taken care of Len's macular degeneration, and mine, and we joined the Foundation as volunteers. Fel and Flora enjoyed sitting in the porch, facing the Sudbury. Meetings, fund-raising programs were occasionally held at Boston College through the courtesy of Dean James Woods.

In Framingham, we joined the annual music fest at the Methodist Church, to which neighbors Dave and Julie Rundlett belonged. Tina sat for their children. Len also joined the Coffee House Choir with Dan McCue. For many years after retirement, the two attended meetings at Boston College, tried area restaurants, especially Irish pubs.

The Sons of Mary had a program in Pasay for street children and in Paliparan to help women learn livelihoods. When I was home, I visited their Pasay location. Fr. John Murphy, on his free time, went to Manila bookstores, pulling my books out so they would be visible. He loved pancit, Intoy's specialty. Fr. John Wallace went with us to the Carmelites and met Sr. Teresa/Pin Constantino. He celebrated Mass there. The Sons' second location was near Malacañang. One night the Sons watched helicopters hovering above, not knowing that Marcos was being airlifted to Hawaii. People Power had won.

Based in Framingham, their Mission House was the site of Filipino gatherings which Cardinal Sin attended when he was in Boston. Fr. John Coss would come over to help Len trim the trees in the backyard. Len gave him red leaf maple saplings to plant by the Virgin's statue. Br. Eugene De Lauro and Fr. Wallace would come to sit by the Sudbury. It was a place made for retreats. Br. Kevin Courtney continues the Mission, after the final priest, Fr. Bob Rivard, passed away in May, 2024.

Boone Schirner's Friends of the Filipino People organized protests against Martial Law. With Filipino groups from other States, we held protest placards across from the White House. The Schirners loved suppers by the Sudbury River and we had supper with them in Cambridge. Raul Manglapus, Heherson Alvarez, Charito Planas attended the Friends' meetings. Raul accompanied Len on the piano at Josie Bunuan. Len knew the Tagalog songs by heart. Another time we stopped at the Manglapus house, after a protest in DC. Ate Pacing lifted up a box of crabs over her head and brought it to the car. She was so down-to-earth.

We were members of the Movement for Free Philippines. After Aquino was shot at the tarmac on August 21, 1983 Filipinos gathered at the Aquino house across from Boston College in Chestnut Hill. I never met Ninoy. Though he was supposed to be a UP Law classmate, I only read about him in the newspapers. My Malabon cousin, Remy de Jesus Reyes, having visited the Aquinos on Mt. Alvernia Street, called to tell me Ninoy wanted to meet me, was thinking about an Aquino biography. I told Remy I only do historical novels and Nick Joaquin would be a better choice. After Ninoy's assassination, Len and I joined protests in the Boston area. One time Raul and Pacita Manglapus joined the group at

Professor Josie Bunuan's house. We could only be accommodated in the basement where lunch was also served. Corazon Aquino remained upstairs and had to be served lunch in the dining room where people went up to greet her. Raul and Ate Pacing remained with us in the basement.

I was invited to join several writers' groups in the Boston area. The Boston Authors Club, the oldest continuing writers' group in the country, was founded by Julia Ward Howe and friends in 1899. Julia wrote "The Battle Hymn of the Republic." Her husband, Dr. Samuel Gridley Perkins, established the Perkins School for the Blind.

George Amadon was a B-29 pilot during World War II. Arthur Walworth who attended the first Red Sox game as a boy, wrote the book on Woodrow Wilson. Wilmon Brewer was the celebrated poet of Boston. His wife Katherine came to meetings with him. While the trustees met, she would lie down on the sofa, in her winter coat and boots. She sent members Christmas cards of family pictures. When burglars stole the Oriental rugs in their Milton house, she said beaming, "I can now see the floor!" Margaret Dunn and I took the trolley to Boston from her house in Wellesley, unless we got a ride from Evelyn Wolfson who always passed by Julia Gardiner whose husband had been consul to the Philippines in the '30s. Julia had lovely memories of Cebu, and treasured the fans I brought her from the Philippines. Her name had an "i", the Boston Brahmin way.

The PEN Women, Wellesley branch had members from area towns. The Working Writers met at each other's homes. So, I learned to drive to Weston, Wayland, Concord, Cambridge; even Boston. Katherine Hall invited me to join the group. Betty Lowry was a travel writer. Betty Hodges was related to the two Southern gentlemen who went to England to plead the cause of the South during the Civil War. She remembered seeing cattle being run from Boston, through Cambridge, to the slaughter house in Watertown. Ev Wolfson wrote about American Indians, had the meadow beside her land plowed and wildflowers sown. Harriet Sibley, 80s still played golf. Pat Richard was born in Chicago and wrote poetry; also, a medical book, *Epilepsy, A New Approach*; lectured on Architecture and Design. Nita Regnier married Jerome Regnier from France. She and her husband lived through the World War, the unrest in the French colonies. Jerome was a member of the Atomic Energy Commission, built their house on an island in Canada, did wall hangings that were exhibited at the Boston Public Library. Nita taught literature at MIT, had in their house an actual computer, one of the first, as large as a piece of furniture. Marcia Seawall was from Dorchester, the old Boston. Patty Wolcott and Nancy Poydar were well-known for children's books. Patty loved my Haviland dinner set which I bought, a few pieces at a time from an antique shop by Hagar Pond. The owner said he would have given me a good price if I had bought the whole set at once.

All those activities actually helped me write. Not focused nervously on the writing, I unconsciously processed my notes until the story or chapter was ready to be written. I knew when: when a first sentence occurred to me in the midst of pulling weeds, cleaning the house and other chores, I sat down to write, letting the words guide me to the end. All that was left to do was to revise, later.

Len and I were active members of the Framingham Library, were members of the Framingham Arts Council. Len gave lectures in several area libraries, as well as the Framingham Library.

We had family time: day trips to Rhode Island, Connecticut, Maine, Vermont, New Hampshire; longer trips to Upper New York, Canada, back to Wisconsin. On the way to Gloucester, we passed by Miss Rose Nelson's Wayside Book Service. She was always so gracious, happy to see us and take the list of books we wanted. Writing us as soon as she found them, she always asked about Gretchen and Tina. Almost every town then had a bookshop of old books so we were able to acquire many books I had earlier borrowed from Widener.

We went downtown to Boston to rummage through Good Speed Bookshop. At Brattle Street Bookstore Mr. Glass, the owner, was often on hand. His son is the Book evaluator of the ongoing Antiques Roadshow on PBS. One time, the Tall Ships were in town and crowds were everywhere, I decided to stop at the Brattle Street Bookshop on West Street, after a writers' conference where the editor of *Atlantic Monthly* Michael Curtis, reminded me to keep sending him stories. The ones I had been sending were too fragile, he said. I was browsing at the tables when one of the bookstore staff came over to tell me a man had followed me inside and was watching me. "Stay inside until he leaves and I will walk you to the trolley stop." He waited until I boarded the T for Riverside where I had parked. I don't recall if I thanked him.

We visited the Caspers in Fond du Lac; Larry and Ginny in Tennessee, Gretchen in Texas, Iowa and Michigan; Tina in California. Len loved to drive, so I attended a Feminist Writers' meeting in Montreal when the organization chose *Awaiting Trespass* one of ten best feminist book of the year. We also joined pilgrimages. Twice, Josie Bunuan led trips to the Holy Land, stopping in Spain to visit Santiago de Compostela; next time, we stopped in Italy to visit Assisi. Josie's sister, Sr. Ignazia, was a Daughter of St. Paul. Fluent in Italian, she did the Vatican radio broadcasts from Rome for 17 years. We visited the Daughters of St. Paul in Rome. With other Sisters, Sr. Lucia, Superior of the Order, came to Framingham. She asked to see the church of St. Paul in Cambridge, liked the Sudbury River and fried lumpia.

And we returned to the Philippines several times, taking advantage of Pan Am's offer of free stops at nine cities. Thus, Gretchen and Tina saw Hong Kong, Singapore, Bangkok, Greece, Turkey, Iran, Spain, Italy, Germany, France, England; returning again and again to favorite cities. In Bavaria, from the tour bus we saw a man who was the spitting image of Len's father. In Spain, finding out I'm Filipina, the guide demonstrated Catalan dance steps and showed us Jose Rizal's cell.

Each time we returned to the Philippines, we renewed old friendships in UP, Ateneo, Philippine Normal College. Playwright Severino Montano invited us several times to his home in Quezon City, once greeted us in costume. Gretchen loved to play in his garden. He sent Len several of his manuscripts and they were in correspondence for many years.

There were conferences at the UP. One year, not expecting us to be in the Philippines, Franz Arcellana on meeting me in UP asked me to be resident fictionist. The scheduled writer had not come. Another time, he inducted me into the UP Writers Club. The first time, I stayed in the UP dorm, returning to Araneta after the day's session. I roomed with Connie Alaras. Together, we went to Mass early. When she came to the States, she stayed with us and we took her around Boston.

Home, we stayed in UP/Diliman, or Araneta, or with Baby in Marikina; we visited Hermy in Pansol where we met Senator Jovito Salonga in our early morning walks; Bella in

Santa Cruz, Laguna. Bella took me to Vigan, just the two of us so I could take pictures of the old churches. When Bella came to visit Vincent and Nancy and Patrick in Boston, she always brought me pastillas de leche. Baby's family stayed with us when they came to the States. Len took Romuel, Raniel and Bella's son Michael to historical sites: Gloucester and Plymouth, Point Judith in Rhode Island. Renald and Mom enjoyed Radcliffe where Mom had a fellowship in the Publishing Program.

After they retired, (Dad as Operations Manager of the Philippine National Railroad; Mom as Chief of the Elementary Grade Division of the Bureau of Public Schools) Dad and Mom visited us for two months. Dad particularly liked Faneuil Hall, walking down to the King's Chapel past the cemeteries. We took them to Concord to see Thoreau's house, which Sr. Bernetta Quinn, Len's Wisconsin classmate also asked to visit. Dad still knew by heart Wadsworth's poems. They enjoyed trips to Rhode Island, Western Mass, New Hampshire, a bit of Maine. Neighbors asked them over for coffee. We took them to visit friends from the Philippines, invited friends over to meet them. Dad enjoyed the river and backyard, kept the lawn free of leaves, as he did in Malabon. Once having noticed twin apples on a twig, he planned to bring them back, but the day they were leaving, when he stood on a chair to reach up, the fruits fell out of his hand and broke apart against the chair. We later planned to go to the Holy Land but health issues intervened.

Len was invited to conferences outside Manila, so we visited Negros, Iloilo, Cebu, Zamboanga, Bicol. Gretchen remembers being at a beach in Iloilo, where she cut a foot on a coral reef, and Virgie Moreno poured Madame Dior perfume on the wound. She remembers going to Virgie's house and seeing cavans of rice in the entresuelo. One night, having brought Hernando Ocampo home, we had a flat tire. Tondo had a reputation of being a place to be mugged so we were wary when the men at the corner stood up to approach the car. Without a word, they proceeded to change the tire and, after they were done, shook Len's hand but did not take the money folded in it. "Bye, Joe," they waved, smiling. It's the kind of memory Nanay would want remembered.

Len continued to encourage my writing. I had written short stories while waiting for the Bar results. On my last day at Harvard I wrote a short story, "The Longer Ritual." Len read each page of the stories and novels. He typed and xeroxed them. He packaged and sent them out with accompanying letters to editors. He was even happier than I when I got published. One time, receiving my letter about the University of the Philippines Women Lawyers' Circle Incorporated (WILOCI) meeting—I was in the Philippines—he wrote back:

Do you still feel you have to compare yourself? I feel sorry if you do. You are unique—if underestimated and under rewarded. You will probably affect the country in the long run more than law practice might have. I know better than anyone else how well you write. What kind of knowledge and insight and craft you bring to your "fictions." Of course, you can't expect recognition if you don't cooperate, at least minimally with someone as sincere as Frankie Jose when he offers an autograph party or something like that. There's nothing dishonest about such an effort, especially so modest a one. I know you are a writer whatever else you may be; and that you write well, if too meticulous perhaps. (September 7, 1980).

... I am awful glad and proud about Dread Empire. *You are the author I never could be, but far from envying you, I honestly take*

pleasure in all your works ... since I know how hard you research and how deeply you contemplate .... I talked with Bonnie Crown, and she is genuinely excited about Awaiting Trespass *... we also agreed the manuscripts should be retyped ... since that would run over $200 if someone else did it, I offered to do it myself .... It will be backbreaking and eye boggling and time consuming, but I believe it's worth it and I offer it as my Easter gift to you .... I reread the novel and it is fantastic. I wanted to take extensive notes to satisfy the promo materials she wants.* (March 29, 1982).

... Typing is tedious, but it allows a prolonged meditation on your novel which can stand that ... I can see why typing tired you. (April 3, 1982).

... At noon, I am on page 160 ... 200 in the new format. I figure a total of 260. Typing is where I can be close to you now. (April 8, 1982).

... Great news from Djerassi ... you have a residency ... congratulations .... Tina and I will manage somehow ... ten years ago you were a Radcliffe Fellow, and some good (if not all you deserved) came from that. So do leave Plaza *with New Day; and do keep after* Whale. *Don't waste your time on things someone else can do.* (March 21, 1984).

... today I read as much of Wings of Stone *as you have written, and it's good. Sometimes, I have access to your best self—your most mature insights and feelings—as you write. (Perhaps that gives you most access to yourself as well.) And I am glad/proud to be your husband .... The faults I found (or marked) in the manuscripts are minor: too much repetition of the time overlap in the first several chapters, considering that this is a major motif and will be picked up later in variations, maybe*

too constant a double-name reference to Rose Quarter-Sylvia Mendez, and not enough recollection of Johnny's experience as a professional.

But your greatest strengths are there, as usual: the deeply felt characters and the suspended pace; which allows surprising information to be introduced just at the right time—especially a knowledgeable way of ending chapters: a short story writer's trick. Johnny (once his professional dimension is added) is convincing, including his seeming sentimental/emotional attachment to Sylvia until she, too turns out to be complicated and worth considering. The father, in his silences, seems more profound than merely shadowy: how they miss each other regularly (and will this have anything to do w/the mystery of Johnny's birth?) is moving. So are Rio and his ghetto people. So even is Martin wholly conceived. You have exposed the rich-and-irresponsible before but Sylvia and even Martin are fresh portraits. One can conceive of them as existing in the same society with Trespass *and* Garden; *and, still they are distinguishable, personalized.*

The texture is less descriptively rich than Telly's, but I think this is close to Johnny's sensibility. Yet at key moments (often with Sylvia) the right metaphors arise ... this novel, like Empire, *depends more on understatement. Yet it is unique in some ways by having several plot lines going on simultaneously—drawing in internal crises (characters) as well as on external events .... How it will end I don't know. But there is already so much substantiality, it doesn't matter.*

Do you wonder why it means so much to me, needing to be loved by you—held in high regard and special regard—when I realize how very special you are, in these novels? (June 2, 1985).

... Although I read making punctuation corrections, etc., I think Book 1 *moves well. (*DreamEden). *Benhur is somewhat too sad to stay with him too long; but the mailman is there, Sally Vergel, Osong, Mig and Joel, to help break the first 100 pp away from pure melancholy. Then Sr. Madeleine! Brilliant. And after that, an introduction to Cayetano*

(who, I presume, will end the novel) and Patro (her 30 pp too long without a break? Anya and Patro's mother-in-law; fine scene): the vaciador (always great) and the Osong party with word of the coup. Proportion and pace I haven't been able to assess perfectly, yet they seemed ok to me. As long as something/someone of interest has the readers' attention ....

Only occasionally were there stumbles, and always from the same source. But this is a novel about "the people," I know; fine; but sometimes too many people are mentioned in the same breath; without adequate identification. I had to figure out who Lola Sula is because everyone's a lola and because you don't give her a name when she's first mentioned, chapters before the third from the end. So, she just has to be given a name sooner and the reader be reminded who she is, later. Almost the same with Anya ... and in the first part of Patro's section, it took too long to figure out that Cleofas was the husband, Demetrio the son ... easy to remedy. Just be kind to your reader ....

But the impression I get is that these 232 pp are polished ... and I'm anxious to read the rest .... Now for the heart of this week's experience. I miss your presence. I miss little conversations with you .... What helps is your manuscript. I have often said that you write beautifully about people, the 100 pages which you left of Stranded Whale *are as good as anything you've ever done (though different of course from your contemporary pieces). I think the 9 chapters are so readable because you had large characters to draw on and because each chapter is virtually self-sustaining: not quite as complete as short stories, but filled with detail, movement and suspense. And you have orchestrated the narrators in masterly fashion, and together they move the historical background forward. Aside from miniscule changes in punctuation, the only negative "complaint" I can make is that I think each chapter needs, at the top, reminder of where the location is .... But if each book can be kept to 100 pages, this should be the best in your trilogy of the late 19th century. I couldn't be prouder as the dedicatee, if I had written these pages myself* (November 24, 1992).

PART 2

GRANTS AND CONFERENCES,
READINGS/TALKS

L-R: Robert Penn Warren, Linda Ty-Casper, Leonard Ralph Casper

1956 – HARVARD

We were still in Manila, so Len sent letters on my behalf regarding grants to Harvard, Yale, Michigan and a few other universities. Yale extended the scholarship grant another year, so I could apply after Harvard, but the commute would have too been too far. Len had an appointment to teach at Boston College, Chestnut Hill, a trolley ride away, so we chose Harvard in Cambridge. The year at Harvard introduced me to Widener where, as a Harvard Officer, I was able to do research for ten years. The stacks were overwhelming. I found at Oceania, D Level West thousands of books about the Philippines. One day, a library staff member came down to inform us that there was a fire, we should leave but not take the elevator. I went up to the 4th floor and saw fire ladders at the windows. It might have been a false alarm since there was no smoke, no later report of damage.

My classes at Harvard were held at Langdell Hall. I registered for Conflict of Laws, Professor Paul Freud; World

Organization, Professor Louis B. Sohn; Juvenile Delinquency, Professor Glueck. The father of Len's Boston College student, Mr. McSweeney, introduced me to the superintendent of the Juvenile Detention House in Roslindale. For the second semester, in January/1957 I enrolled in Admiralty, Administrative Law, and World Order/International Organization under Professor Louis B. Sohn. I recall Roscoe Pound, several times holding the door for me; while through my mind ran his opinions which were held in high regard at UP Law.

Dean Griswold and his wife invited students to tea in their house, sent Christmas cards to each. Professor Brown talked to the foreign students at the afternoon cocktails. There were picture takings. As the second semester was winding down, Professor Sohn offered me a research job for the summer, and I took the trolley to Beacon Street in Boston to research at the World Peace Foundation. Sally Roper and I, among others had applied to the UN for a fellowship. Professor King inquired about the year's appointments. Neither of us got it. But Professor Brown suggested, because of my high grades that I take a year for a doctorate in Jurisprudence. I could not reconcile that with the plans Len and I had already made.

Classmates at Harvard were from Germany, France, Spain, other states, especially from the West Coast. One asked me for a macapuno tree. I explained that macapuno being a mutant, no plant was guaranteed to bear those sport coconuts. Ernesto Maceda, Manila councilor, was a classmate. Sarah Roper from Halifax shared an office with me, in the basement of Langdell. She and I corresponded for years. She urged me to respond to queries for the *Alumnae Directory, 1953-2003* which published my rather long letter explaining how/why I had put my training in law to write historical novels of the Philippines. Here is the letter:

My most memorable experience at Harvard Law was having Roscoe Pound hold the door of Langdell Hall for me. I was speechless each time it happened, for his opinions—which we memorized at the College of Law of the University of the Philippines—were running through my mind.

The most significant thing that happened, which redirected my life, was the afternoon Miss Ryan announced that, because of an impending hurricane, students were advised to go home. Passing Widener on my way, I decided I had better take a look before I left Harvard. I found in D Level West, material about the Philippines I never knew existed. And I discovered how unfair and erroneous were some of the material. So I decided to write an essay refuting these. On discovering that some of the books had never even been taken out, I decided instead to write a historical novel which might have more staying power/life outside the shelf. Just one book, then I'd go on with my life.

As it happened, I have not stopped writing historical novels about the Philippines, starting with *The Peninsulars* which was set in the 1850s, the period of the British Occupation. I went on to the 1896 Revolution against Spain in *The Three-Cornered Sun*. Though the chronological sequence was interrupted by novels set before/during/after the Marcos dictatorship, *The Stranded Whale*, about the Philippine-American War, 1899-1901 (which I also researched while a Radcliffe Fellow) finally came out in October 2002, my 12th novel. (Three collections of short stories also intervened.)

Only after many years, with the UP Law Class '55 (whose valedictorian I had been) having fun designating me the

71

Class "deviate" for writing instead of practicing, did I realize that writing is a form of advocacy. I was defending the country against unwarranted "smearing." And writing is compatible with having a family. With a "room of my own," I ventured out only I want to; can occupy myself mostly with what can be "dropped" when the idea for a chapter or story comes, so I do loosely scheduled volunteer work pro bono.

Awaiting Trespass, which was chosen in 1987 one of the Top 5 novels in the UK by the Feminist Press in London, recently got a "commendation" from a 30-something Filipino. In an "internet review" he wrote, "Those who live their adolescence in the '70s and their college in the '80s value these lines because these were our generation's lines. Reading the novel by Ty-Casper makes me feel so alive—I see pictures of Manila—and the people during my left there."

A paper, read at Ateneo de Manila University as part of an "honoring" this past November, stated that "every Filipino cannot but savor such a world recreated in the literary and historical text of Linda Ty-Casper ... in *The Stranded Whale* ... we ... can participate in the creation of that nation that was dreamed of and fought for one hundred years ago."

These remarks keep me from giving up writing, a very real temptation until some student asks, "Are you writing about People Power II?" "When is your book about the Japanese Occupation coming out?" And friends, relatives send me newspapers, their notes on radio/TV accounts I miss by not being there. I get unsolicited material, too. I was sent *Charles Eliot and the Ashfield Dinners (1879-1903)* by someone who lived in Western Massachusetts. I come upon material in flea markets. All signs I take to indicate I should write at least two more novels to complete the cycle.

If I had not stopped at Widener that afternoon in '57, I wouldn't have found Mrs. William James' clipping of the Philippine-American War (mislabeled "Insurrection" in American history texts), the collection of letters to editors and of soldiers' letters during that War, the Anti-Imperialist material ... I could have saved myself not only the anxieties involved in writing (one can never write as well as one wants; and research is exciting only until it becomes tedious: I have to research as meticulously as I can so I do not contradict history), but also the question that continues to pose itself: what did you do with your training?

In Bangkok, to receive a Southeast Asian Writers Award, after my acceptance speech, a man came over to remark, "Written just like a lawyer!" I guess I put the training into historical novels about the Philippines.

As it turned out, writing historical novels became my life work. Nanay's wish to have her stories written, after many years, became realized.

1963 – SILLIMAN

E d and Edith Tiempo invited me to the Creative Writing Workshop while I was still writing *The Peninsulares*. The discussions, a new experience for me since this is my first workshop, helped me decide to use the material left from the historical novel, for another: *The Three-Cornered Sun*. Some of the writers had been to the prestigious Iowa Writing Center.

1974 – RADCLIFFE INSTITUTE

t was The International Year of Women, and Len thought I should apply. To make sure I did, he asked P. Albert Duhamel, NVM Gonzalez and Margaret Hartley of *Southwest Review* for recommendations. The Director was Sue Storey Lyman, daughter of Moorfield Storey, the anti-imperialist who in 1898, wrote with Marcial Lichauco *The Conquest of the Philippines by the United States, 1898-1925* to protest the annexation of the former Spanish colony that had successfully revolted against Spain, had proclaimed a Constitution, establishing a government in Malolos. Mark Twain, was another anti-Imperialist, who opposed the taking of the Philippines.

My office faced the open space between the buildings, shaded by trees. I rode in to Cambridge with Helen Heineman whose husband John was in the History Department of Boston College. Lunch break was an opportunity to talk with other scholars and writers. Ezra Pound's daughter, Mary de Rachewitz, who curated the Ezra Pound collection at Yale, invited me to Ravenna. Rosellen Brown wrote short stories. Emily Lyle from Scotland wrote about Scottish ballads, lectured in several US universities. When Tina went to London, years later, she visited Emily who with Helen and Julia often came to the house. They loved the Sudbury River. Helen Heineman said Radcliffe Institute was like a monastery, each resident kept to her office.

Once, Len's doctor asked if we could invite Julia to give a talk at the Harvard town library. Julia and Emily enjoyed the trip and the town. Dr. John Whitcomb graduated from Amherst, was in the artillery during World War II, like Len: both had hearing problems. One day, after my check-up, he asked me to schedule one for Len. I told him Len was not due for a check-up. He said he wanted to talk poetry.

Mona Harrington who was at Harvard Law the same year I was, 1957, was one of those I met in Cambridge, along with Becky Karo, and Marilyn Harter who also lived in Framingham. Becky liked *The Peninsulars* so much that she treated to lunch in one of the small specialty restaurants in Harvard Square. Back in Framingham Marilyn, Helen and I exchanged visits for many years.

Gretchen helped carry books I borrowed from Widener where she also did research for her own papers. We enjoyed the small specialty shops and restaurants tucked between buildings on Brattle Street. Tina was intrigued by the padlocked room at a corner in the stacks at Widener where artifacts of Theodore Roosevelt were kept. She loved going up and down the stairs at Radcliffe Institute. Olsons delighted them. Calliope had children's clothes. Down towards Boston there was 10 Arrow where we got a birdbath made by an artist from Pennsylvania. Too good to put out we placed it in the fireplace. There was Oona's, a shop of "experienced" clothes, where some racks were out on the sidewalk. In the Square itself was the Wursthaus which Len particularly enjoyed. And a French restaurant another street up. After his classes, Len picked us up near Loeb Theater so we would not have to get on the trolley to meet him at Boston College. Waiting at Loeb Theater, Tina would get a Fresca and a bag of sour cream potato chips from Sage's.

The Radcliffe Institute grant gave me years of access to Widener, as an Officer of Harvard University. Years later, at the library the first line of *Awaiting Trespass* occurred to me. I couldn't get past the first paragraph, until after lunch, back in the stacks, I chanced to describe the casket as closed. That set the stage for Martial Law. It took me years to revise. Readers' International of London published it in 1985. Bonnie Crown who had started sending out our manuscripts said Sherman Carroll read it in one sitting in her office, decided to take it and asked for another book. I was still writing *Wings of Stone* which he took after reading it in one sitting; and asked for another. I had started writing *DreamEden* then. *Wings of Stone* and *The Transparent Sun* which Alberto Florentino published as a Peso Book, was about the only manuscript of mine that didn't get rejected. *A Small Party in a Garden* which I wrote after *Wings of Stone*, was published by New Day because the foreign publications were too expensive for students in the Philippines.

1984 – DJERASSI

Julia Budenz, who was there the year before, suggested I apply: she said residence at Djerassi is just right for writing in one's room, alone. Len who has been to Stanford encouraged me to apply. He would take care of Tina and CCD, Girl Scouts, ballet, piano. It's only a month. Len convinced me.

Up at 5 a.m., Len and Tina took me to Logan Airport, Boston with my red Hartman bag filled with notes, on the 1st of November, Friday. NW Flight 159 left Logan, 8:20 a.m. I had a bulkhead seat. At the San Francisco airport, Eric Houts met me, 6 ft, beard—description he sent—with Ian, 20 months old, in a stroller, "talking" about his boots. The Foundation car went up Route 36, with the Bay on the right. The day before, someone came from Hawaii.

Skyline Drive. Beautiful, winding up. Peregrine falcon, red-tailed hawk, deer. Bear Gulch Road rose higher. Narrow, abrupt turns. Past redwoods. Rounding the hill, about 40 cattle, calves just two weeks old. At the crest, a view of the ocean through breaks in the hills. Trees only in the gullies. Sculptures moving with the wind, like insects large on stiff legs. Groups of rocks above which, clouds; and higher still, hawks.

Last gate at the end of the road: Djerassi. Eric showed me the Artists' House, my room: a desk, double bookcases, a bed, a bureau. Through the deck, a small redwood that looks like a tamarind. Sky. Then Eric pointed to where the fire-fighting equipment are. Fire is a hazard here.

I hang up my clothes, called home: 3 p.m. here; 6 p.m. there. Father John has just said the evening Mass at St. Jeremiah.

Tonight, the Djerassis will welcome the residents. A lot of strangers. I will be one of them. Len will be at evening school. I'll call him tomorrow. I sit at the desk, write to Len and Tina, Sister Teresa and Father Cawley. It's cold. If I can last here, I can last in Maine.

Just Carl's son Dale and his family came, with his mother-in-law, a member of parliament. I met Carolyn Wong from Hawaii, who's on her first book, *The Story of my Father.* Edit Sorel is from France, Laura Schiff from Berkeley. Lenke Rothman is sparky in a low-profile way. Ann Hankeman is a composer. Steve Vincent a poet who laughs deep but not really listening to anyone. His shock of gray hair makes me think of scrub oak. Tom Lindsay is bubbly, is voting for Mondale. Steven Vincent knows Len's friend Bob Peters, a poet also from Wisconsin. I can already tell who will be good to listen to.

November 2; up at 3 a.m. Read the Missalette, said the rosary and went out for a walk. Foggy. Can't see the ocean. The cows lifted their heads to look at me. One has red hooves. The calves are frisky. Prickly peppers—identified in the laundry room chart—and Rayolite reflectors dot the road. A break in the fog, an impossibly beautiful sky, as if everything is just being created. Back in my room I rewrite Chapter 1 of *Stranded Whale*.

I called Len and Tina who are out. Gretchen is writing her dissertation in Ann Arbor.

Laura drove up to the crest to show Edit, Carolyn and me the sunset, the Throne—two large rocks pushed together, overlooking the other slope of Carl's hill. He owns 1,400 acres, worth $375,000 per. Sculptures with their own shadows, some with chimes that compete with the wind. She said, Pami Djerassi is buried at the far end of the grounds. The Foundation is named for her.

Edit and I discovered we both write in longhand. We won't wake each other with our typing. She knows eight languages.

1,012 steps uphill. Stellar jays, black and electric blue feathers. Tanagers. Frogs in patches of water on way to the Barn where the Dutch sculptors live. Carolyn walks with me. She says, Katherine Ann Porter reminds her of me.

Carl Djerassi comes with a contraption on which to rest his leg. He's 61, white hair, short. He talks briefly about Marcos, said Julia Budenz sent him her book of poems. He's an optimist, re Mondale's losing. Things turn around. Edit said everyone has to read into Carl's machine, for tax purposes. She read her piece in French for ten minutes. We will take turns.

Laura goes to homeopathy for ringing in her ears; the doctor prescribes a powder. Must not touch it or its power is lost. May I use this for a story? Yes, she says. She uses her friends' and they like it.

The first line and title of a story came to me, and facing the hills, I sit in my room to write "Hills, Sky and Longing." It's day seven. Laura gives me a copy of her fairytale in Hungarian which she wrote here. "Once upon a time, there was, there wasn't, and if there wasn't why should I be telling you there was a gypsy boy named Shurny who had a violin!"

I called NVM. Last I saw him was 15 years ago. Long talk about family, writing. Narita is taking arts lesson. Before supper mailed card to Helen and Julia, Sr. Mary Helen. Sue Flynn is chef, used to be in publication. Nothing fazes her, not people in and out of the kitchen. Some nights we are on our own or we volunteer to cook. I have made pancit and liver pate, Jello salad.

Wednesday, 8th day. Will go with Sue Flynn to Palo Alto so I can see Stanford where Len met Mom, Fel and Amador in '51. I think of Mom walking about the campus, missing us, as we missed her. There is a Christa Cross over a doorway. I didn't take a picture. Some 30 years ago, it wasn't there.

Back over Skyline Drive, descent so steep. I had mailed postcards for Carolyn. For myself to: Tina and Len, Ate Luz, Ruth and Rose, Dr. Saul Radovsky, Burton Raffel. After supper, back to Chapter 3. Both Laura and Edit, and Carolyn have read *Dread Empire*. Carolyn gives me a copy of *Lament of the Lady of Ch'in* about the sack of a city in the 880s. Rest. *Polyphoenix* tonight. Can I last four hours? Tom will reserve seats.

Saw the Coit Tower coming and going. Back by 11 p.m. Tina and Len called yesterday, 6 a.m. here. Call Tina and Len tomorrow. Sunday. No one goes to church here. Tom is a Protestant, Edit and Laura Jewish; Ann a lapsed 7th Day

Adventist. Carolyn? I'm Catholic. I can expunge my sins, Laura said.

Sunday, November 11. Mysteriously, a newspaper on the table. Will rewrite to lift up the draft a bit. Rewriting is harder than the first draft just flowing till it's done. When the first line comes to me, I never know how it will end, how far it will go. If it will stall ….

Edit wanted to go to Miramar. Laura took us, down Bear Gulch to Skyline Drive, to Route 35, Magellan Road. Ann will drive herself. Stop at Dr. Frederick Aquaviva, holistic dentist, Christian Counselling and Marriage. Stone Maiden on the way.

To Princeton, past Bach and Dynamite Society. Laura treated to octopus. Bring your own beer. Edit loved the place. Nothing like it in Paris. Jazz. Her enjoyment was absolute. No room for five at Fishtray. Laura suggested Half Moon Bay. Carolyn and I got smoked oysters. Back at Ranch, I made salad, Laura made feta cheese omelet. First time we are on our own. Talk about the *Polyphoenix*. Performed sensuously, French accent. Then a pair exorcised the record by making animal sounds, shooting off firecrackers. A woman who gets loads of new grants pushes a grocery cart around. Tom: You're lucky you did not see all four hours of it.

Then the Jack Daniels. People started to get funny. Edit read French poets/And again/And again/And again/Cette rapture … And again/And again … brought out her scarves to drape over herself, over us … Tom taking pictures … we stuck fruits to the metal sculpture on the wall … lemon crackers, red pepper, potatoes, green onions. Ann posed in meditation before it, with a candle. Laura propped a napkin on her head, a short veil … Tom and Ann read from the Bible. First time we relaxed. Carolyn left, touched too much. Carl didn't think it funny but Tom said, we and the cows are his tax shelter.

Monday, November 12. St. Josaphat, Bishop, Martyr. It rained all night. Breakfast with Laura who was up at 1 a.m., reading a history of Hungary. She sends her short stories to Hungary. She and Edit speak Hungarian. Sue and Carolyn went out to mail letters. They offered to bring my film to be developed. Carolyn will xerox "Fellow Passengers" for herself, and a copy for me of Zbigniew's poem, "Five Men, about World War II." Quite moving. Edit went with Talbot to the doctor in Palo Alto, wearing a black raincoat, black hat, long cigarette. Very Parisienne. I tell her the doctor might be thrown off by her glow.

I work on my manuscript. Laura brought out her traveling typewriter and very good paper, $3 a ream in Berkeley. Called Len and Tina, Veteran's Day. They were both writing to me before going to the Reach Out Concert with Br. Francisco and Fr. John Murphy of the Sons of Mary. Earlier Tina made up piano she missed Monday.

Carolyn read "A Story of my Father," starting from the end. She apologized frequently. Peer criticism of her stories at John Hopkins made her take up law. She practices civil law in Hawaii, was surprised I have a law degree. She types till 2 a.m. Laura hears her. Carolyn is intrigued with Pami whose ashes are scattered in these woods. Pami's poems, 61 pages, *Mother to Myself*, was published by Daniel, Wilbur Springs, CA. Laura thinks after Pami died her parents began to think of her as a real artist, like Sylvia Plath. Ann and Laura talk far into the night.

Tuesday, November 13. Rain. I heard each drop because of the trees, the way it rains in the Philippines. Water collected in gullies. We saw the ocean from the table. Edit said we should go to Big Sur. Took an hour to decide. Lunch, the pancit I made which Laura and Edit like. Tom made omelet. Tonight, Sue will be making couscous.

Reading the short story again. Carolyn wanted to see it. I'm tired of the hills. I want to be home. Laura has been here three months. I now wake up 5:30 instead of 3 a.m.

Wednesday, November 14. Sunrise 5:30. We went to Big Sur. Sue and I go ahead. I sat in back with Ian, his juice, banana and toys. Then Sue strapped Ian behind her so I can see the ocean. Half Moon Bay to Route 1, almost closed because of mudslides. Cliffs impressive. Santa Cruz, coffee at Pangalis. '60s hippie kind. French pastries, macarons, croissants. Snapdragons on the table. Woman tells her child they don't have money for another bagel: eat the oatmeal we brought. She knits. Bookshop.

Laura was angry. Edit thinks she's worried her sore wrist will keep her from doing massage, her source of income.

I thought of Mom at Monterey and Carmel. She sent me a red sweater and pair of red shoes. There is a picture of her in a gray suit, against a tree, smiling. She was younger then, than I am now.

At Nepenthe, Edit treated to drinks. I got rum and cider, ambrosia hamburger. Ian walked into the marigolds. Laura wanted to buy something. The clerk wiped the earrings she tried on, with cotton dipped in alcohol. Gallery on Cabrillo Road. Did Mom come here?

Started back by 2 p.m. Passed San Gregorio Beach which we see from the Ranch through a break in the hills.

Too tired to help Sue. No water at the ranch so Laura made tea with rainwater.

Long straggling evening with Cornfeld, art connoisseur who's interested in the Dutch sculptors, just back from tour of the Southwest. The sisters asked Tom to get Scotch from the Barn. Three inches high drinks. Edit served wine. Ann taught me Urdu. Tom said, I instigate quietly.

Back in my room, read letters from Gretchen and Tina. Tina and Len are going to Sister Anne's Poverty Meal. Len said he finished his panel paper, had called me yesterday.

Thursday, November 15. No water in Ranch. Again.

Worked on Chapter 4. Parroco. Eric knocked. Would I want to be interviewed? He said there were Filipino movies in Berkeley. He knows about Aguinaldo. He asked if I miss my family, if I'm writing in English.

Laura called me to dinner: the pâté I made and Scotch; with crabs Sue brought, half each person, but some managed to get a whole. Try to be content with just enough. Tom did the dishes.

To Barn for Ann's composition. Carolyn came to my room to see the short story I wrote. She finds it hard to say what's on her mind, Tom brought his guitar to the Barn. He yodeled to make us laugh. Laura noticed Carolyn is gone. I found her in the kitchen, walked with her back to the house. Then to bed, holding the rosary Gloria Paculdo from UP Law gave me years ago. Water flowed in the gullies; heard some birds, not owls.

Friday, November 16. St. Gertrude. Thought of Gert from St. Jeremiah. The irises she gave me from her garden are still blooming by the Sudbury River.

Light sky. Laura made tea from rainwater. To conserve, water is turned off at night

Can't write, so just read. Grass now green. Redwoods are propagated by seed, no big cones.

To San Francisco Ann drove with Carolyn, Laura, Mathilde and me. Sjoerd was in SF yesterday and didn't come. She and her sister Mathilde stay in the barn. She paints colors not figures; Sjoerd sculpts. Their uncle, a SVD priest in the Mountain Province, builds roads and works on irrigation for the people. He's about 77. They're from Holland/Netherlands. The sisters built a smokehouse in the Barn; to smoke mackerel.

Passed San Jose Catholic church which has Filipino murals on the walls; pass Filipino stores. Private showing of Pat Ferrera Hope's quilts. Talked about Ifugao communal ownership of land. Anti-nuclear war movie. The dead in first nuclear accident were cut up to remove radioactive parts—to dump with radioactive material before being returned to the family.

Impossible to see the road on the way back. Passed gullies from where men and animals drank in the 1850s.

Will miss Edit who doesn't talk much but listens; will think about her work and feel the magic. Promised to write to her Paris address. Nervous day for her. Laura calls her Gypsy Queen with her headband and full scarf for going out. Her stomach bothers her, no relief from pills. We said our goodbyes. Laura started crying. The quiet of the hills makes it hard to sleep.

Saturday, November 17. Laura will take me to her house in Berkeley, a wood duplex with boarders. Claude from France is selling his Mercedes for $3,000. He's a lawyer. Laura gives the other boarder a massage, $25. Lunch at deli. She treated to Brazilian chicken salad. There is also adobo salad. To downtown. Square Mall with expensive glassware. No Philippine books. Got Ian a book, *The Chicken Who Sails.* Antique shop, more bookstores. Berkeley Student Union.

Laura would not let me share gas, so paid toll. 75 cents! Could see every reflection on Bear Gulch Road.

Carolyn came out, had not eaten. We warmed up leftovers, talked a bit. Laura feeling better about Edit.

Sunday, November 18. 35th Sunday of Ordinary Time. Worked on Ursula's chapter, read Laura's translation of Nin Cassian. Will buy a copy from her. She got 100 copies as royalty. Sat on deck I had shared with Edit after walking. Decided not to move into Edit's room.

Called Dad 3 p.m., Monday there, 7 a.m. Marcos very ill. Might go to the States. Dad sounded good. Talked to Baby. Raniel wants a motorcycle. They sold the new cars Mom and Dad bought him and Romuel.

Laura and I to Stanford, Bechtel International Center for reading of her translation. Stina is a fellow at Stanford Center for Research. Roses in the courtyard. Thought of Mom.

Sunday, November 25. Christ the King. I remember the processions.

Raining. The light over the hill is like a halo. I thought of Nanay's stories about processions. I watched the halo getting narrower, a worn wedding band like the one on her finger. Just another layer of skin. I remember the tray of wedding rings in the Brattle Street antique shop, Cambridge; easily about a thousand in the pile, heaped like roasted cashews sold in Manila sidewalks.

Rain and a bird singing. A red madrona repeating the shape of hills. The sun a soft moon. Olive trees in groups. Redwoods growing out of clumps cut a hundred years ago when sawmills dotted the hills. Rain running down the branches of the redwood beside the lamppost. We walked to the sculptures.

Monday, November 26. To Stanford with Sue. Walked to the Quad, the Art Gallery, Hoover Museum. Cast of Rodin's *Gate of Hell* looked like a lava flow, bodies melted together in a fire. The original is five minutes away from Edit's in Paris.

Wednesday, November 28. Rain, so walked inside; filled the cat's bowls. Stellar jays alerted.

Carolyn typing on the dining room table. Laura took a course on Enneagram on the seven personalities. She thought I'm five: observant, detached, non-competitive, seeks no prestige: the negative qualities of eight personalities.

Don't want to start a chapter. Might not finish it before I leave. So many notes unread in red leather carry-on. So many clothes not worn.

Len called 1 p.m. and 3 p.m. Noel Hughes died. I used to carry her when we first came to Boston College. Each time they moved, the Hughes asked us to move, too. Private service. She was to marry Cecil Tate, also of the Boston College faculty.

Tina called, she's in Honors: A in Math and Social Science. B in English, Spanish and Science. She's getting ready to sit for the Rundletts next door.

Laura and Eric are waiting to see if I'll go to Redwood City with them. Just asked them to buy me some film. Waited for Len to call again re my flight home.

Walked to Barn to see Ann in her studio. Three skylights. Musician's easel. Bedroom in the loft. Walked back to pack a bit more.

Laura asked if I will walk uphill with her to take pictures. Snack on persimmons Tom brought. Then supper. Maiden hair squid pasta. Carolyn didn't come out till we were halfway done, returned to her room immediately.

Almost all packed.

Thursday, November 29. Laura asked if I would like to make some paper but I'm going to Palo Alto with Sue and Carolyn. Laura suggested, on my return, that we walk to the picnic grounds, a trail we have not taken, near where Pami's ashes were strewn.

Stanford Museum of 19th century art. Rodin's bronzes. Portrait of Leland Stanford, wife and son. Tissot's paintings. Keith's panoramic landscapes. Replica of golden railroad spikes. Pomodoro Cube given in memory of Pami. Stanford. 1971.

Back at the Ranch 3 p.m. Sue too tired to go on the trail. Eric, Ian went with us. An old logging trail. Feel of darkness and shadows. Mushrooms. Large redwood roots cross the trail. An owl. Another owl. Deep gullies. Stumps out of which new trees are growing ... a feeling of going where one has been.

Sue followed. It's the last day for me. She and Eric are the perfect couple.

Rope and wood sculptures, like witches from an enchanted forest. Swamps. Mushroom inside a log. Took picture of Ian looking into the log.

Picnic grove. A single plank across a creek, newts moving dreamlike, red bodies, orange underside. Banana slugs, fat and yellow. An owl hoots. Only 3:30.

Sue and Eric returned to the car outside the gate. Laura, Ann, Carolyn and I went on to old logging mill. Ferns, moss, turtles, a little waterfall, a sculpture of wire. Laura said, "Here is where Pami's ashes were strewn." We pause.

Then over a creek, a gulch. Cliff on the right. Deep ravines. Maple with large leaves. Larches. Wild iris. Strawberries. Shamrock. Downhill walk after uphill.

Ann saw a bobcat. More owls. We each placed a rock over reindeer moss and twigs, promised to meet here three years to the hour: 4 p.m. Dead or famous or unknown.

We came out by the old Barn, uphill. Redwoods darken the trail which narrows. A magical forest. Ann will compose a piece for the occasion.

The Barn is like a painting. Slow upward plodding. Wide tracks. Back at the bridge. Poison Oaks need sunshine, too.

Moon on water holes cattle hooves have dug. A thousand frogs croaking.

Someone called from the tree with six trunks. Eric with a flashlight, first-aid kit. We all walked uphill from the Barn to the Artists' House

Ann cooked Indian curry. We all pitched in. Laura cooked cabbage, onion to transparency, to mix with noodles. Seven places at the table. Afterward, we sat on the floor. Making the night last. Ann and Eric talked about his work. A work-fest. Laura sews a book of her fairy tales for me. She'll sketch me for a page in it. Carolyn read *The Three-Cornered Sun*. Sue read to Ian who fell asleep, woke up to play, and fell asleep again. He still likes the book I got him.

Coffee. No time to call NVM and Brother Francisco. Laura massaged Ann.

We exchanged addresses. Carolyn thanked me for letting her xerox "Hills, Sky and Longing"; for comments on her work. She is torn between writing and practicing law.

Almost 1 a.m. We all go to our rooms.

Too tired to sleep, I packed some more. Then picked up Gloria's rosary, packed it, too. I dreamed, perhaps or just got lost in thinking here is where I am old, unloved; and loved and young again.

Friday, November 30. No sunrise, no rain. I'm not sorry to be leaving though I'll miss the hills, the friends I made here.

Laura worked on a book to keep me company. Ann came out. Then Carolyn. No talk. Just being in the front room, together.

Sue and Ian came. Eric has errands so she'll take me to the airport. But Eric came, took my bags to the gray station wagon. Goodbyes, Ann, Laura, Carolyn. Sue said she'll load slowly and drag, so we can say goodbyes, surprising me with feelings she has not shown before.

The sky very clear. The hills, ridged with light. A falcon flew within a yard of the windshield. I saw the talons. Eric said that's good luck.

We talked about writing. He wrote a historical fiction, set in the Chicago Exposition ... an old woman looking back at her life. He and Sue and Ian will go to Princeton by the Sea where we had chowder, once.

I'm thinking of the moment as past.

Eric took my suitcase to the check-in counter. We said goodbye, hugged, promised to send news. They are a good couple with unusual dreams which I hope come true in the best way.

Walked to Gate 53. Not a long walk. Asked for seat near the front. Saw the Bay as the plane lifts up. Sand as flat as snow-covered lake. Seagulls. Stewardess put the heavy carry-on with my notes in the overhead. Left 11:45 a.m.

Flying time to Minneapolis: 3 hours, 15 minutes. Reno on our right. Snow-capped mountains. South Dakota on the left. The earth looked so far away. Snow showers in Minneapolis. Gate 26. Two and half hours to Boston. Cruising at 33,000 ft. Tail wind will get us there five minutes earlier. 51 degrees there.

Len and Tina at the Gate. Tina held flowers: yellow mums, orange tiger lilies wrapped in paper.

1990 – WHEATLAND CONFERENCE

In January I went home. I had called Dad who said he's
waiting for me so he can check in at the Kidney Institute.
He had also waited for me when he had to go to the Heart
Center; and the Lung Center. Len and I figured January 24 to
March 7, based on previous hospital stays.

Very cold, the river frozen across. I had baked Russian
tea cookies, a chicken relleno to freeze, for Tina and Len while
I am gone. I make lime pineapple cream cheese Jello, which I'll
make for Dad when I get there.

Ready to leave: typed the Daily Mass schedule for Lent,
gave Irene Colonna the $74.73 in the treasury. Will not have to
miss Memorial Mass for Marianne Lordan. Jackie Reichert
brought candies for Dad. He loves Butterfingers. Ceil Wohler
had a farewell dinner for me at Wayside. I attended meetings
at PEN Women Wellesley, Boston Authors, the Workshop. I
put the chapters of *DreamEden* on my desk, to return to when
I got back. Len will read them, after he writes a

recommendation to Djerassi for Greg Brilliantes. Tina will commute to Boston College, babysit on weekends.

Last call to Dad. He wants a pair of Florsheim shoes. I called Gretchen. Len and Tina take me to Logan, 5 a.m. From Chicago, 13-hour flight. Cruising altitude: 39,000 ft. I have three seats in back with Pertierro's *Religion and Political Reality in a Philippine Community*. Arriving, I give Dad cologne, Polaroid films, the Florsheims, the cookies I baked, the candies from Jackie Reichert. He looked weak. At the hospital, Tita Tuazon, resident physician and friend from Boston, checked Dad. Also Drs. Chavez and Danquilan. I will stay with Dad in the hospital.

He passed away March 7, the day after I left, telling him I would be back soon. That evening, Ate Remy Banez and Lirio said Dad lifted his arms, "Linda pull me up." I went back March 9, for the wake and funeral; stayed to take care of the arrangements, the bills, the paper work.

In the plane I think of all the things I could have done for Dad, held his hand while he prayed in Spanish which I could not follow; talked to him about Calbiga when he was restless. I wonder if he really needed all the transfusions, the tubes to clear the lungs. When he pulled the oxygen tubes out, I could have talked about what we would do when he got better. Forty days after Dad passed, the first line of "Tides and Near Occasions of Love" came to me. Steve Bautista of the UP College of Law, told me he knew Dad had died when he read the story in the *Philippines Graphic*.

So, I had fully forgotten the Wheatland Conference until they called to ask about my flying arrangements. Nancy Fitzgerald helped with that. Len and Tina urged me to go. The cardinals are in the apple tree. It will be all right. Called Gretchen who will come while I'm away. A Wheatland representative met me in San Francisco. Reception that night. I met NVM and Narita Gonzalez, Frankie Jose who must have recommended me for I had not applied.

Wheatland International Conference: mostly European writers with name recognition. A competitive air at the conference that I'm not used to, since I rarely attend them, except with Len. Writers tried to occupy the space of the big names that had not shown up. NVM said: We write for noble ideas, not for recognition. No expectations then. Just enjoy my large room at the Stanford and the solicitous care by Nilda, who's from the Philippines. We talked in the room between meetings. I gave her a copy of *Awaiting Trespass*. I am her Ate.

Reception at the Getty's. A dinner at Sausalito where we are so busy talking in the elevator that no one pushed the button until someone wondered why we were not descending.

The third day, I gave my 7-minute talk. "History, and Literature/Women Writers: Babaylans." I wrote it on waking up and spoke without notes, since I had just written it in longhand and remembered. The staff said it was good. Christopher Hope said the talk was good. They are surprised? The editor of *City Lights*, Ferlinghetti asked for an article, saying I was the best. Antonin Lechin, *Lettre Internationale*, asked for a short story. He's moderator of the Central European panel. Miyoshi invited me to give a talk in San Diego, but there is no time. Signed copies of *Awaiting Trespass* and *Wings of Stone* for Jess Cabrera, a Filipino doctor.

NVM and Frankie decided I would be spokesperson for our panel and give the summary at the last meeting where a woman writer asked to change places with me so she could talk with the publisher of *North Point Press*, next to whom I had been seated. Writers strut about from table to table. NVM said, "Let them. We know our worth." Wearing Luisa's light purple dress, I felt no need to strut.

I had my hand kissed twice: by Syed from Russia and Georgian Amisejib. Harrington translated for them.

I returned home on Dad's birthday, June 16. I had written "Happy," set in Muir Woods, named after John Muir the environmentalist from Wisconsin. The story is about Sausalito and the redwood trees watered by the coastal fog, its tap roots reaching only 13 feet deep, and a young woman renouncing her family roots. It ends with her looking up at the sky for the star that came to life when she was born; remembering, that her mother said there is such a star.

Wheatland ("Happy") and Djerassi ("Hills, Sky and Longing") were the only two places where I wrote a story. I'm glad I went.

After Wheatland, 40 days after Dad passed, I wrote "Tides and Near Occasions of Love." Sr. Bernetta Quinn, Len's classmate from the University of Wisconsin, heard it being read on BBC. It had won the UNESCO/P.E.N. Prize in London.

Sister visited us once, taking the bus from Minnesota. She wanted to see the site of Thoreau's hut on Walden Pond. She was at Bellagio years before Len and me.

Thinking of her, I remember the little boy from the village below Mount Tabor walking up to the fence to give me a yellow flower, like a buttercup.

1993 – THE SOUTHEAST ASIAN WRITERS AWARD

October 6, Wednesday. Len and I gave Dumas grapefruit peels before we left the house, placed the pot of sampaguita on the porch table; left at 5:33 a.m. to catch the 6 a.m. Framingham bus. A ridge of red in the sky as we left. Driver whistled old tunes. Most houses still dark. Forgot the Bengay for back pain.

Len and I left Logan 8 a.m. on NW 161. 6 hours to LA. 7 ½ hours to Bangkok from LA. Approaching LA, mountains took over from the desert. Wagons skirted these mountains on their trek west.

Left LA 2:30 p.m., Thai Airlines, Royal Orchid. Seats 9J and 9K. Might work on 3-minute speech. Idea for short story came, but not intense enough to be insistent. Kristina will be going to Mass for us.

Seated in upper deck plane. Very courteous service. Too stuffed for a second meal. Read article on Buddhism. In contrast with traditional focus on merit, heaven/hell ... focus on gaining insight into state of all being, interrelatedness:

suffering, dynamism, the non-self. To let go, give up emotional affinities, prejudices, illusions; get back to pure state of mind, scrub from the mind layers of attachment/sense of self ... compassion, respect toward others, animals, nature ... Duty in life, to use our best according to our role, place and time, without selfishness and greed. Spiritual immunity to materialism. Social work part of spiritual duty, to bring to reality a community life, in harmony, free from suffering. Buddhism, Hinduism merge in Thai religion ....

Stewardess called us by name. Wine, champagne with dinner. Didn't get wine.

Flying over heavy rain clouds. 10 ½ hours aboard. Rim of light as at Haleakala. Snow-capped Mt Harmon? Time is parceled out among memories. Tina so wanted to come.

Stewardess kisses my hand on way out. Hug her. Delay with connecting flight.

October 7, Gretchen's birthday. Arrived midnight in Bangkok. Rosary for Gretchen. 3 a.m. Texas time. 7 p.m. here.

Arturo Reyes from the Philippine Embassy met us, delivered invitation from Ambassador Rosalinda Valenton Tirona, for Sunday dinner.

Hotel desk receptionist wide awake, took us to our room. Hand garlands. Fruits from General Manager of the Oriental Hotel, Kurt Wachveitl. Drew back curtains to look out on Chao Praya.

October 8, Friday. Finally fell asleep 7 a.m. Up 8:30. Talked with Carol Martin at Embassy.

10:30 a.m. Press Conference, Regency Room, Oriental. Seated next to Prince Diskul. Met president of Thai PEN. Strange to have proceedings in language I do not understand.

Awardees from Singapore, Indonesia and Malaysia do not understand Thai, said their language has more similarity to Tagalog.

Lunch. Lord Jim. About 50 dishes: lobster, filet mignon, pasta. Prince Diskul teaches art history.

2 p.m. Press Conference, The National Library auditorium. A lot of questions, President of Thai PEN showed me *PEN Journal* with "Tides, and Near Occasions of Love." Questions about it from moderator. Difficult to read: comment. A lot of students. Journalist from *The Nation* asked questions. A woman gave me a bag of Thai suman. At the landing, a Thai turoturo served fried catfish. Temple of Dawn.

Back by boat to the Oriental. Rest. Snack brought to room. Carol Martin came to the room.

By boat to Terrace across from Oriental, wearing Mom's blue saya, hand painted baro and sash. My books didn't get here from LA. I'm supposed to present Xerox copies. Kurt Wachveitl, General Manager of the Oriental, sat with Len. He's from Bavaria from where Len's father came. The Prince explained the dances. Devils and Monkey dance. Awardees received envelopes. With 35,000 bhats. Salfrida said even fake gems are expensive. Mom has given me star sapphires, and other gems. I don't know what to buy.

Took hotel boat to the reception. A lot of river traffic. Hotel courtyard, orchids growing on trees as in Araneta. To Authors' Lounge. Authors' suites up the twin staircase. Bamboos reached up to second floor. Tinted glass roof of courtyard, below our rooms, effect of a forest canopy.

October 9, Saturday. River cruise on the Oriental Queen to the Summer Palace. Lunch on board. Breakfast on veranda with Ramadan and Salfrida from Indonesia. Then by bus to Ayutthaya—second city of Thailand. Guide said there should be a book on Thai/Philippine relations; said rice fields were being sold for factory sites, proceeds spent on cars, appliances. Soon farmers become homeless, become contract workers: Japanese economic colonialism. King Rama V had traveled to Singapore, Philippines. The King's brother is the father of Prince Diskul who presided yesterday.

Singapore, Indonesian and Malaysian awardees conversed in Basa Malaysia. "Puting Bato" has same meaning to me.

Ayutthaya was twice captured by the Burmese who burned down wats to melt the gold. A wat commemorates a Thai victory. Old Palace. Present King goes there to pray before trip to Burma, apologizing for the necessity. Queen is very ill, rarely seen except in photographs. Memorial to wife who drowned on way to summer capital: rowers could not touch her to rescue her. Gothic Wat nearby. Beautiful buildings.

Lunch aboard the Oriental Queen. Tourists from Germany, Spain. Waterlilies, but not as clogged as the Pasig. Muslim sections of the river. Barges carrying rice, sugar, sand; almost as large as a royal barge but without decorations.

Guide, Kwan, resented losing the rice fields—used to be green all the way to the horizon, islands of trees mark villages, monasteries in larger villages. Assistant professor at Thomassat University, she feels changes erode tradition and culture. Send her Len's book and mine. Too many loud Japanese who, Kwan says, cut down Thai forests for chopsticks, leaving their own forests intact.

October 10, Sunday. Mass, Assumption Chapel, a minute walk from Oriental Hotel. Beautiful statue of Our

Lady, side altars. Len brought our hand garlands to the altar with St. Michael, Holy Family. Rain after Mass. Girls who closed chapel talked to me in Thai, sounds Chinese without the harshness; offered me an umbrella.

Breakfast at Verandah. Waiter suggested I try Thai omelet, like Ninang's.

Write copy of talk for Mala, xerox front and back of book for His Royal Highness Mahavajeralogkorn.

Lunch overlooking river. Rest. Too tired to shop. Ramadan said they have spent their check.

No klongs which I recalled from past trips to Bangkok. Hotel car to Jim Thompson to look at silk. Everything more expensive than in the States, even picture frames.

Dinner: awardee's own embassy. Ambassador Rosalinda Valenton Tirona arrived with Ruby Parial who remembers Len and me from UP, where she was in Social Work, knows Sonia Gandionco Mathay. Here from Vienna, Ruby is originally from Gapan. The ambassador is from Talavera. Carol and Jun Martin. Ambassador, in Burma three years, wrote book about the posting.

Returned to Oriental with Ambassador Rosalinda Valenton Tirona, Philippine flag on side of hood of her car. Round of goodbyes, Filipino way. Ramadan and Salfrida were not met at airport, no arrangements from their embassy.

Traffic over bridge reminded me of traffic around Quezon Circle, which Dad and I watched from his room at the Kidney Institute, while we talked when he could not sleep.

October 11, Monday. View of river during Rosary. Pineapple slices at 4 a.m. Breakfast. Veranda. Eggs Benedict. Lunch at Thai Airways International. Wore Mom's brown batik saya with her tambourine. Didn't take turn at simulator in plane. Given gifts: wall hanging, cards. Sat with wife of Brunei awardee who hardly ate, didn't speak English. Nitaya of Thai PEN talked with Len. Across, Supatana, Oriental Hotel P.R. Hotel has staff of over 1,000 for 323 rooms. No tour groups.

Quick trip to market to get lanzones, with Salfrida. Got two round batik tablecloths-brown and blue. Back by bus to hotel; his HRH went by Mercedes.

3 p.m.: Reading room opening. Wore national costume: Mom's blue saya which Leni Gonzales trimmed for me. The baro sleeves and sash are hand painted. Packaged books to present to HRH.

Woman in charge of the room welcomed us. Met the women from PEN Council who attended the first dinner. Kurt Wachveitl, a real gentleman, sat with the honored guest, Lord Jeffrey Archer.

Dinner: Seafood Market, host Rich Monde went to AIM, Ateneo, wants to go back to the Philippines. Sat with Vladimir Bunoan from Vigan. Only Len of the non-Asian foreigners attended, sat with Kurt Wachveitl and the critic from Malaysia with whom Len had great conversations. Brunei, Malaysians, Indonesians, Singaporean, Thai. The Thai awardee gave us copies of his books (wife is a linguist).

Letter from Frankie Jose asking for one-page report for *PEN Balita*. Crown Princess had visited Solidaridad Book Shop and her children's books were translated into Pilipino and published by Solidaridad.

October 12, Tuesday. Lunch at Verandah.

Reading room to write 3-minute talk, read it to Len. Not perfect, slight variations during the talk will improve it. Arkana is in charge of the Reading Room, is President of Thai

PEN, Writers Association. Nitaya Masavisut is PEN president. Rested instead of shopping.

Rehearsal at Grand Ballroom at 3 p.m. Tucharin gave set of instructions, with diagrams. Another man showed us how and when to curtsy. Not too low. Supatana bends her knee like a genuflection. I will do a curtsy, not a genuflection. Will wear Josie Bunuan's black saya which Pitoy Moreno, Virgie's couturiere brother designed for her.

Such a flurry. Chanchou Bunnay asked me to deliver speech in English not Tagalog. Lord Jeffrey Archer said, "Be practical. Use English."

Tea in Authors' Lounge.

6 p.m. Embassy Room. Philippine Ambassador Tirona, Carol, Ruby. Sonia Cataumber-Brady, Zeny, Adrian, Arturo—ten kababayans attended.

HRH late, headed for the "throne" seat; shook hands with foreigners, not with Thais. Our gift-wrapped books rested on round trays. Attendant, kneeling, brought the trays to HRH.

Dinner. Len seated at the Philippine table. I sat across from Kurt Wachveitl, Ramadan on my left. Menu on gold cloth. Champagne toast. Anthem played.

We walked down, every step preceded by a bow or curtsy: Accept award, three curtsies. Step back, three curtsies.

Gave three-minute speech. Philippine contingent polite, restrained. After speech, big applause, a lot of book signing, including Supatan, head of PR. I was asked to give a lecture. Many young students asked for my signature. Long line. Photo with Lord Jeffrey Archer after audience with HRH.

Packed before going to bed.

October 13, Wednesday. Up 7:45. Last breakfast. Went to Library. View of Chao Praya. Wore Mom's batik saya for tour of Grand Palace. Brought umbrella Len got me from Brett.

Guide, Prince Diskul who wrote book on the Grand Palace. Brunei awardee's daughter married someone from Tarlac. We shared the umbrella. I remembered the first time we went to Bangkok, a woman offered Gretchen and me a branch to shade ourselves from the noon sun.

The Emerald Buddha is really jade. Lord Jeffrey Archer as appointed spokesman, thanked HRH.

Lunch at Bangkok Bank. General Manager and Executive VP said she has children in the States. His Excellency asked me to be spokesperson. Spoke about what literature can do: when governments distract the people from the issues, literature can provide the information to combat political lies. Information in literature can empower. Literature lives on beyond its last lines. Carol had speech xeroxed for Malaysian journalist. Missed cocktail party at Author's Lounge

Farewell dinner. We entered the Jim Thompson House to find everyone standing at their places. Kurt called to us, "Please come to the head table." His wife Penny seated next to Len, then Lord Jeffrey Archer, Thai awardee and wife. Kurt said my speech was the best.

The awardees' wives were surprised I did not strut, though I spoke English. We exchanged addresses, they promised to send me batiks. Very warm goodbyes. We will miss each other. Kurt reminded Len we are welcome to the Oriental, any time.

October 14, Thursday. Departures.
Up 3:30 a.m. Only $12 in bill. Everything free. Double-tipped. Goodbyes again. Len took pictures. Left 5 a.m. Only

25 minutes to airport. We were escorted to the Lounge. Exchanged 20,000 bhats for $784; somehow, I lost 3850 bhats. Taxied out 9 a.m. To Seoul, 2 hours ahead of Bangkok. 10 ½ hours to LA. Another meal 4 p.m. Bangkok time: smoked salmon appetizer and entrée, Champagne, dessert. Read some of the gift books. Ambassador Tirona, on saying goodbye, said, "Keep your citizenship." My intention. My promise to my father. LA, 70s. Not checked, should have kept the lanzones. 3-hour wait to board for Boston. 4 ½ hours direct flight. Boston very pretty from the air. 11:15 at Logan. Framingham 1 a.m. No frost apparent. Still bright by the rock. But Crown of Thorns is brown. Gave Dumas a bath.

1994 – BELLAGIO

L eft the house 11 a.m., March 2, Wednesday. Moderate snow. First in line at Delta counter Boston. Hip and leg hurt, sharp pain in lower back due to arthritis and sciatica. Took one Voltaren pill before boarding at New York. Cleared through to Milan. Hard to sit with pain in the leg.

March 3, Thursday. Arrived 1 p.m. at Bellagio. 7 a.m. in Framingham. Assistant Director, Gianna Celli met us and showed us our rooms.

Perfect stillness. From the bedroom and study, beautiful view of the Alps and Lake Como. Latin name, Larius. Pliny the Younger was born in Como. Their Bellagio villa must be where the present Serbelloni Villa was built.

The Serbellonis were from Milan. For centuries they had access to the highest power: papacy, monarchy. Cecilia Serbelloni married Bernardo Medici, 1498. The region abounds in saints. The first 20 bishops came from Como.

Mussolini came to Como. Mona Lisa might had been painted in the area of Lake Lecco.

Lunch. Met Pasquale Pesce, director. About 12 of us. Pink gardenia centerpiece from the garden. Framed tapestries as in our room and study. Met Jim Anaya, Carl Hovde. Len registered passports. Our study has view of the Alps, snowcapped. A perfect stillness. 3 p.m. here is 9 a.m. in Boston. Tina is taking Statistics exam in Framingham.

March 4, Friday. The mountains looked different. Took pictures with help of Kofi Agavi who was in transit at the Manila Airport when Ninoy Aguino was shot on the tarmac. At breakfast, met Frank Toker, Bob Stewart and Margaret Brower (music), Christianne Pappon from France, Wayne Brown from Columbus, Ohio, whose poems are forceful, Maria Adair, artist from Brazil. Her paintings are on exhibit at Bahia, and Paris from where she gets her canvas. She paints quickly, two a day. Ellen Green is from Boston, speaks Italian.

Seagulls outside our window. Another Voltaren. View of Lecco side of lake. Olive trees and cypress to the edge of the lake. The hills are like those in the Mona Lisa. Daffodils. There's a large vase of it in music room. A picture of Mrs. Walker who acquired the Villa in 1980, lived there until her death, leaving an endowment.

Third floor reading room, library. Started Nin's Chapter and Baler detachment. Revise after typing. Len has mastered the typewriter in our study, has written description of his project. He xeroxed a map of the Villa, and a page of the Philippines from a 1933 French encyclopedia. He got new folders, IBM ribbon in town, with Tom who got medicine.

When I thought I couldn't write, a chapter started: Nin with detachment in Baler, 3 pages. Will type and revise. Leg stiff.

Lunch: salad—cold cuts, fruits, potatoes, olives; spaghetti, cauliflower, grilled beef and chicken.

Dinner. Len at head of the table, with Carl Hovde and Christianne, Minos Tzanakakis who's working on pests attacking olive trees. Elfriede is working on a painter of Greek vases, was in the Philippines eleven years ago to look up the Baroque churches. Gianna said her husband, Roberto Celli, passed away a year ago, former director.

March 5, Saturday. Wrote two pages after breakfast, frequent breaks to look at the lake, both arms visible from the porch. Slope of rhododendron and red magnolias. From the hallway, view of Mount Blanc. Took another Voltaren after breakfast but leg still stiff. Tom Gaisser has sciatica and back problem. Len said his book on cosmic radiation is more poetic than those in *New Writing*. Julia Gaisser is a classicist, has book on *Catullus*.

Break for lunch in small breakfast room: Riso Arancini alla Siciliana and salads. Minos, Carl, Len, Pasquale Pesce. About Mrs. Walker, charmed by the restaurant the Villa had become, asked for the bill, expecting the price of the Villa to be included.

Minos is from Thessaloniki, quiet but with deep opinions about politics. Politicians use divisions about Macedonia and Yugoslavia to excite constituents. Wrote possible pages for *Siege of Baler*.

March 6, Sunday. Heard the bells from the towns along the lake. Len went to look for the monastery up the hill. Olive and cypress trees remind me of Galilee, the building in the shape of the Cenaculum in Jerusalem. Then as prayer, started typing; way of connecting, of being grateful to be here. Len walked down to the lake.

Lunch was fish, ravioli, polenta, grilled and stuffed peppers, eggplant. Conferees of AIDS program here. Sat with Margaret Stewart, composer. Her husband, Robert is also a composer. They have apartments in both New York and Virginia. She offered to teach me the computer in ten minutes. Christianne Pappon is working on a novel and a book on women in politics. At the first dinner she wore her French Legion of Honor badge.

Typed after lunch, have some 20 pages which I will revise. About 4 chapters from *Siege of Baler*, to interpose among the chapters.

Called Gretchen and Tina before supper. Gretchen is glad we're here.

Supper in big dining room, Robert Stewart's birthday. No speeches. Just champagne. Crisp tablecloth and heavy tableware.

After, a time of quiet, questionings. Dormition Abbey … in stillness, without words ….

March 7, Monday. Dad's fourth anniversary. He wanted to go to the Holy Land and Italy. Rosary, since I can't walk down to the church I can see from the window. Angelus, another rosary.

Mist lifting up. Men already working on terraced slope. I can see what could be grottoes, a greenhouse that looks as old as the hills or promontory. Azaleas.

Breakfast with AIDS conferees. At lunch, Louisa and Ron who said Kidlat is a film maker he most admires. Couldn't recall the last name; only that Kidlat/Lightning was from the Philippines. Ron is doing a critical study of a black filmmaker of the '20s who made what was then known as "race movies."

Lunch: pastry with eggs, broccoli stems, fruit. Coffee in veranda. Len walked to Montserrato to take pictures. Elfriede's son from Munich came for the day. They walked around, tasting buds. Read in the Library, instead of coffee. Hour for meals: end is announced by serving coffee in column or music room, or veranda. Breakfast at our leisure.

March 8, Tuesday. Watched the blue truck coming up from town, bringing bread from the bakery. Asked for bacon and shared with Gaissers. Irene asked about novels about the Philippines to make the country real to her students. She teaches about street food—the MacDonald fast food of Third World countries—has been to the Philippines: Iloilo, Manila.

Then to the Library. While our rooms are being cleaned. Typed first Chapter on Baler, 9 pages became 11. Then, May 1 naval battle from Federico, Fermin, Andres' viewpoint.

Lunch: salad with prosciutto, pasta with broccoli. Irene's birthday. International Year of Women. Talked about feminism, demonstrations, result of carcinogens in soil and air, experiments on soldiers and citizens conducted by governments. Switzerland dumps nuclear wastes in Italy which dumps it in Africa.

AID conferees. Wore black floral dress with black jacket, seed pearl earrings. Bill said, optimistically, it will take 50 years to rid the world of AIDs. At least eight strains of the virus discovered in North Thailand, spilling over into seas, Burma, China.

To Library. Wayne took out both copies of *Awaiting Trespass* and *Wings of Stone*. Ellen went down to Lake Lugano, by ferry to Menaggio, back to Lugano. Pain in my leg kept me from going with them. Two Tylenols, plus Voltaren, hot baths and heating pad.

March 9, Wednesday. A week ago, we left Boston.

Breakfast. Gianna Celli is angry about corruption in Italian politics. She has been in Bellagio some 20 years. Len and I shared bacon and omelet.

Walked down short steps leading to town. Len took pictures from the front door with the lions, then he went on to Santa Caterina, and I returned to the Library. Len discovered film not turning in camera. So must retake pictures. Then he'll try to figure out the washing machine. Then take pictures in the music and column rooms.

Lunch in bigger dining room with Julia G, Mill Walker, Ron Green, Len, Minos, Pasquale, Robert S. Talk on deconstruction. Gnocchi Romana, white beans and turkey. Rested instead of joining coffee hour. Mist covered view of the Alps. Tiramisu very good. Two Tylenols.

Retyped Baler Chapter. Letter from Tina, sent February 28. Upbeat. Genetics and Stats tests over. Try to restart Manila Bay Chapter/*Stranded Whale*.

Jim Anaya on indigenous people and their international law rights. Then dinner with conferees. Margaret said she feels Telly's sadness and loneliness. She received best teacher award in Virginia while she was here, not anxious to leave. Jorge Barrientos from Chile/World Bank. Didn't join coffee. Len and others ignored sign dinner is over, continued to sit and talk.

March 10, Thursday. Gianna will take me down to the lake for Maria's Open House at Casa Rossa. Near docks at Pescalla, the stables with big round posts of basalt. Then I typed 6 pages of Manila Bay. Not my best but I have something to revise.

Before cocktails, Margaret Brower presented her composition, then Frank Toker on excavations. There's a notarized account of the first Mass said by the Bishop at Santa Reparato, Syrian name for churches with no name, no relics. She's leaving tomorrow. Elfriede leaving tomorrow, too. She and Margaret gave me their cards. As post war student in Frankfurt, Elfriede helped carry away stones from bombed city. Wore my white piña Philippine outfit.

March 11, Friday. Took pictures of Elfriede beside camellias. Saw Margaret and Robert off, then the Tokers, then Jim Anaya. Tonight, Elfriede and Kezia. Looks like rain. Forgot it's Friday and had veal medallions for lunch. Will not go to coffee and cake to make up for it.

Laundry after lunch. Machine so noisy. Tom Gaisser, whose room is next door, came out. Receptionist called the maid who said it's normal. Ironed.

Typed handwritten versions of Baler, threw out old versions. Typed Battle of Manila Bay Chapter. Collate information for next chapters.

Dinner with Pasquale and Piano Foundation, re concerts at the Villa. Talk about hazards in Ohio, Massachusetts. Milledge Walker has been to Indonesia. Minos wife, Egli, is arriving from Greece.

Elfriede left before coffee. We all clapped. Liqueur in Music room. Talk about going down to bar in Bellagio, getting a taxi for me.

Wayne Brown talked about difference between him who grew up in Trinidad where blacks are the majority and run the government, and American blacks. Hot bath, then Tylenol.

March 12, Saturday. Pictures of residents in drawing room. Those before 1984 are in Princess Room upstairs. Len walked to Gate A. I went as far as grotto, before the bust of Serbelloni. Didn't dare go as far as Montserrato—Tom's study. Too far.

Iced leg. Typed page 7, Battle of Manila Bay.

Lunch. Christianne and I asked for less spaghetti. Brought my orange to study. Pressed a camellia …. By 5:30, 14 pages. Missed tea and cake again. Very misty. Carl went to Como, misty there, too.

March 13, Sunday. Len walked to church at 10 a.m. Stayed in Library with Donna and Julia who's reading *Awaiting Trespass*, says she is enjoying it. Donna said Wayne's family are value-oriented aristocrats of Trinidad, never gained/regained wealth. His father is a judge. She asked where I get my clothes. She has been to Boston, Filene's Basement.

There's a bust by Leonardo da Vinci in the Library. A Cranach in the breakfast room. Discreetly placed cameras in both rooms.

Lunch with Christianne, Louisa and Len. Talk about Duras … Christianne asked Len for list of American authors. Sat with Irene at far end of table. Pasquale said he likes to cook; has a 17th century recipe for pizza which started out as dessert, not entrée. Irene asked him personal questions. He's from Naples, family in Rome where he used to direct the Stanford program. Degree in aeronautical engineering.

In afternoon, sorted my notes. Then a short walk to Serbelloni bust, statue of Pan with skin of leopard/lion. Montserrato is too far for me to walk even with my cane. Dinner: sat with Maria who said Brazil music Pasquale played is not from the Bahia but Janeiro. Different beats.

March 14, Monday. Worked while maid cleaned room. Plotting chapter after Manila Bay, the June 12 Declaration of Independence. Decided to bring the character of Victor Arvisu from *Ten Thousand Seeds* since it would be logical for him to have been at that place, in that time.

So hungry. Ate cashew while Len went to Bellagio for postcards, stamps, aspirin. An hour back and forth. Washing machine is broken.

Lunch, duck and pasta. Pheasant last week. Mill is planning a trip to Bellagio/Bergamo today. About eight in a van: he and Irene, Julia and Tom, Carl, Maria, Len and me, if I can make it. Christianne using movie camera during coffee, overlooking Lecco.

Leg hurting all day. Rested. Got up and wrote 1 1/2 pages before dinner. Then Ron's presentation on Michael and race movies. Then cocktails. Then dinner. New people arrived. Dinner, Len and I at head of table. Julia, Carl and Minos at our end. After dinner drinks. Talked with Ingga who translates into Danish. She and Claus built a house in Almeria, go back and forth. Claus writes 3-4 books a year, poems, novels. Well-received in Denmark. Wrote his first book at 25, autobiographical poem. Went to Princeton after WW II. Suggested we keep Bellagio a secret.

Maria said I'm gaining weight because I don't move around much. She said I should go to Bergamo. Sunny today.

March 15, Tuesday. Minos's presentation on olive tree pests. Diapause/quiescence. Wendy said, men in NY in sexual diapause. She used to think gin was perfume.

March 16, Wednesday. Len and I make our presentation. Reading room. 6:30 p.m. Many questions. Read Victor Arvisu/Terio Salazar Chapter. This is Paradise. Is it possible to be bored? Rose said she got bored in church when she was growing up.

March 17, Thursday. Donna is putting Wayne's interviews with AIDS participants in computer.

March 18, Friday. No breakfast but got picnic lunch for Bergamo. Gianna suggested warmer clothes for church interiors are cold. Sat with Julia, Tom.

Long drive around Lecco. Suspended figures within circle of steel, chapels. Lower Bergamo. Museum has a Velasquez, portrait of Tiepolo. Tom, finding the steps too high, suggested I take the lift. A Nativity, Mary's household with rabbits. Got a catalogue. Then to the city on the hill. Picnic lunch on Mario Lupo Street, with Maria, Mill and Irene. I'm glad I went.

March 19, Saturday. Letter from Tina re her thesis. She works hard. We might go to Tempe in December to visit. She said their bikes were stolen. Called Dora: last week, 6-8 inches snow.

To Library with Donna. Then lunch outside with Maria, Ingga, Wendy, Paul C and Paul M who asked how Joker Arroyo got his nickname. Paul Carrington has been approached by sugar planters from Negros about recovering losses to Sugar administration, knows bankers in Philippines. Typed Stephen Mullis Chapter/ Cavite Viejo/powder magazine. Then back to reading index cards.

Tea and tart with Minos, Mill, Irene. Didn't watch Bocce game down by Maria's studio. Ron Greene showed 1925 movie *Body and Soul* with Paul Robeson. Conference Room. Ron will tell me how to get Kidlat Tahimik's films.

Claus, with Ingga, said I should go to Copenhagen and Switzerland to see his doctor who cured him. He gave up painkillers, take wine instead. Soaked in tub instead of joining after-dinner drinks.

March 20, Sunday. Breakfast in room where Cranach's portrait hangs on wall. We all—Minos, Len, Carl, Wayne—asked for omelet with bacon. Then walked to wall past bust of Serbelloni. Len took pictures of Santa Caterina. Pressed flowers for Gretchen and Tina. Past statue of Pan to look down on ruins of a fort. Seagulls. Said rosary, sitting on bench.

Carl and Len had aperitif in front of camellias. Read Claus story about plague on Bergamo, powerful like a Bergman movie. Publisher, Fjord Press, Seattle. Conference on Refugee Children. Donna kept the day's menus. Her last day.

March 21, Monday. Finished Victor Arvisu Chapter. Typed 8 pages. Carl gave us his card, also Minos whose wife Egli is arriving today from Greece. He'll take ferry to Verona, train to Milan, bus to Linate. American secretary is from Providence, Linda.

Lunch inside with Paul Moravia, Len, Irene, Mill. Had seconds of spinach and cheese rolled in crepe. Dinner, chicken/rosemary, baked Alaska. Maria painted Tom's tie green. She paints chairs.

Conference on Refugee children. Paul played piano before presentation of Women in Politics by Ingga.

March 22, Tuesday. Lots of picture-taking. Carl Hovde, Wayne and Donna left. Pasquale joined us.

Walked to San Francisco and Santa Caterina. Rosemary shrubs being trimmed. Rose bushes between rows of evergreen. Knee and leg hurt. Len went down to Bellagio to get three Murano pendants and postcards.

Christianne left with her brother who came from Nice. They'll stay in Pescallo tonight. She said to write her if we'll be in Paris. Kissed us before leaving. Coffee near the auricaria and camellia. Photograph session before the camellias: Claus, Ingga, Len and me, Ron, the Gaissers, Irene, Maria. Cold. We all had coffee. Wore my Philippine outfit.

Paul Moravec's presentation. CD used 200 tracks. Background, church bells from his Anglican/Episcopalian youth.

March 23, Wednesday. Len got another tree Murano pendant and owner gave him a second one without his asking. Most shops still closed.

Breakfast, Minos and Egli came, then the Gaissers, Ron and Luisa, Irene and Mill. Gideon and Aliz ordered ham. Carl Hovde was usually first at breakfast, got us to order omelet, bacon. Irene and Mill met in India when she was writing on the first elections, the toast of correspondents. She said Mill could accept her giving her career priority, having taught in Shanghai. Taught at several black universities, ended up in Berkeley where deer feed on their shrubs.

Paul Carrington: law as training in ethics. Lincoln came out of the woods with a great soul, Charles Summer had the training Jefferson envisaged—law can uplift souls—but had no soul. Legal training not necessarily better than apprenticeship.

Ashokamitran doing his literary biography. Said, All your burdens are in your heads, inside your own eyes. Your eyes don't seem to look outward at anything…your eyes turn others into images of yourself. Your mirror is a distorting mirror … full of self-pity … all your sorrow, all your difficulties are because you are so poor within yourself … you have so few resources. What can the poor receive from the poor?

He and his wife carried water in containers to their third-floor apartment at home. He was afraid she would feel isolated with no Tamils in Bellagio. Said Post Office would sell him only one stamp at a time.

March 25, Friday. New tables in breakfast room. Pink tablecloth. Vittorio would not let Len take his picture in his waiter's uniform. Len took picture of chair Maria gave Pasquale. She showed slides of her early work and development to painted chairs and sticks. Presentation in Conference Room.

After dinner, stood by fireplace in drawing room. Minos came over, said not to delay seeing a doctor when we get home. Or maybe, see specialist in Switzerland as Claus suggested. Said he has had a bad back, two bad shoulders treated by a cousin in London. X-ray didn't find problem. Wendy M has tendonitis in her arm but doctor didn't recommend X-ray. Without Donna, no one to remind me of tea.

March 26, Saturday. Breakfast 7:30 a.m. Gaissers, Ingga, Ashokamitran. Elections. Pasquale going to Rome to vote. He said Kennedy came and stayed during Dean Rusk's tenure; arrived by helicopter near Sfrondata. Revised Chapter on Capture of Manila; from Philip to Terio or Victor angle. Too many facts cluttering. Put appropriate index cards with typed pages. Threw out yesterday's version. Leg hurts. Read on Malolos Congress.

After breakfast, Len went with group to Cadenabia, Villa Carlota. Minos and Egli went, too. A lot of villas on Como and Lecco. Tea: Pasquale with architects to design Frati, Capuchin chapel with fresco. Group went by bus, then hydrofoil to Como: too far for me. They went to the Duomo, back by 5 p.m.

Dinner in breakfast room. Grilled lamb/chicken, zucchini. Sat with Mill. Egli. Ron who enjoyed my tartlet.

Too cold in terrace which overlooks the lake. Wore brown Benetton turtleneck from Len. Claus said I should throw out my notes and just write; drink wine instead of taking painkillers. He does not use computer. Ingga saves his work into the computer. Mill said month limit on residence to avoid hanky-panky. Turn clock ahead tonight. Night on Bellagio. Len went with Minos and Egli, Kerry, Wendy Lamb, Gaissers, Maria, Pasquale. Pasta for second dinner. Three bars and restaurants: Top, heaven; middle, Earth; bottom, Hell.

Everything in the world has a beginning, an end.

March 27, Sunday. Only Len and me up at breakfast. Had ham omelet which Len didn't want. Then to Princessa's room near Library. She has two portraits there, one young, another older; a man's portrait across her desk with white chair in alcove facing Lecco. Sailboats on Lecco. Like a painting.

Egli and Minos went down to Bellagio to watch procession. Len to church 10 a.m., lit a candle. Missed tea and cake. Green loose jacket and Evan Picone blouse. Wistarias covered with flowers. Camellias, too. Len, Minos and Egli came up from Villa Melzi, passing by bocce game near the waterfront.

Material too big to tame into a chapter. Still on Malolos Congress. Bring in Surigao/Agusan/Bicol. Long rest, then one small movement at the desk brings back the pain. Shark oil for leg from Raniel.

March 28, Wednesday. Laura and Ron gave us copy of Klaus Riflejerg's *Witness to the Future*. Read it in the Princess Room. Finished it by 12:30. Len went down to Bellagio to get more films. Man sweeping camellias flowers on ground. The foundation employs five percent of town. Women in Islam conference.

Len took pictures of Egli and me in Princess room. Read Chapter on Women and Insanity in Wendy's book. Talking to angels/feeling of being damned. Golden delusion/delusions of grandeur, positive self-image could be caused by venereal disease.

Back on Malolos Congress, Simeon/and Heraldo/La Independencia, municipal governments. Check Federico/Andres Chapter on war/revolution.

Irene's research on invisible street food in Iloilo. She thought I can go to Vara by boat to see the villa. Talked with Paul M's friend who'd doing research in Switzerland about Joseph Conrad.

Dinner with women from Muslim countries. Amel from Sudan. Wore Gretchen's black dress with Algerian jacket.

March 29, Tuesday. Far right won elections. Gianna hoping for the Radicals. Old money went to Berlusconi. Breakfast. Yellow and white flowers, mimosa and daisies.

Niehls Lynne: Power used against the weak. Nail time with work: the time it takes to create will always be yours ... time does not end but it has passed. Not much to life actually .... Time is passing while I'm thinking. Keeps on passing. Nothing so wretched as being an artist ... struggling, grasping at something that can't be grasped ... no amount of effort will help me reach it, even if I slaved until blood bursts from my fingertips .... A soul is such a fragile thing ... no one knows how deep a soul goes in a human being. You should be good to yourself .... A human can become whole by living. The Lord has no interest on our cleverness here on earth. We can never completely remove that God from Heaven ....

Len went to the Frati. Took pictures of courtyard. Capuchin burial ground, Casa Rosa, stairs to Pescallo.

Started Chapter of Jacob in Malolos; deliberation on Constitution. 4 pages to revise. Leg stiff but not painful.

Lunch. Talk on Berlin Wall, aftereffect. Claus sold 20,000 copies of his book on E. Germany, before Wall fell. Karl said you could tell an East German right away.

Gianna said she'll take me around tomorrow. She's sorry I miss going down to the town.

Sultana Kamal of Bangladesh said problem of Filipina Moslems is not primarily living under Islam but living with Christians. She's a lawyer, working on women's issues. Gideon: I see you get along with the Muslim women. Marienne is from Algeria but lives in France, started the network in 1984.

March 30, Wednesday. Framed Chapter of Malolos Congress: Jacob, Aglipay. Conscience and soul.

Misty but no rain. Vittorio said this is the longest stretch of good weather.

March 31, Thursday. Reworked Jacob Chapter. Breakfast. Sultana gave me her card. Egli gave me prayer beads from Greece because we're their closest friends. She showed me the pink/white/blue Murano necklace Minos got her. After Bellagio, Minos and Len corresponded until Len passed away in 2018.

Lunch. Sat with Claus, Ingga, Egli, Karin and Joachim. Len went to get earrings and three hand-painted birds.

Maria's Open House, Gianna took me. She said the tip goes to a common fund and is given to Linda Triangolo. Gave individually earlier. She talked about the trees—cypress/fingers of God; sour cherries, pomegranate. Maria giving postcards, almond nougats, cookies, cake. Claus and Ingga bought bathroom painting. Len took pictures. Bocce: Rex, Bessie, Gianna, Tom. Crushed stone court. Boccetini/little piglet. Farida, Sultana, Marienne came. Ashokamitran came.

April 1, Good Friday. Up 6 a.m., looked at the lake, grounds. Breakfast. Red blood orange juice, plain omelet. Lingered. Wendy, Ron, Luisa with Minos, Egli, Karin, Goden and Aliza, the Gaissers, the Carringtons. Gianna. Hug from Karin who got out of taxi. Gave Rajih $20.

Villa car came on time. Everyone at front door. Goodbyes again. Leg throbbed on ride to Malpensa. Too misty to see Villa Serbelloni after first turn. Bellagio from lower gate, town stores, produce and candy. Ferry. Park. 1:45 minute ride.

Goodbye to Julia and Tom who shared Villa car to airport. Said to remind them to Julia Budenz. They gave up their suite for us, so I could be near shorter staircase, and roomed at the tower.

Checked in at Delta. Still have 47,000 L. Save for Gretchen.

Plane detoured to France. Two-hour delay; ran out of pills. Took last Voltaren with juice and pretzels. Tylenol after lunch of pasta and cheese. Pain did not subside till after six hours. Dora had brought our car to bus station. Home. Dumas on Len's chair.

Sorted mail. Up till 3 a.m.: 9 a.m. in Bellagio. There is life after Bellagio. I am grateful for recommendations from Frankie Jose, NVM Gonzalez and Burton Raffel.

1996 – TEXAS A&M

April 13. Texas A&M reading and talk on invitation of Larry Reynolds. Introduced by Jane Stout. Faculty and students attended. Remark: Joe Gelson said the talk was moving and charismatic. Met Margret Ezell.

1998 – PHILIPPINE CENTENNIAL

August 1. Philippine Embassy: no visa needed if Len staying just 21 days.

August 7. Left Boston 8:30 a.m.; in Chicago 2:05 p.m. Leave 5:20 p.m. for Manila.

August 8, Manila. Raniel picked us up. Stayed in Marikina with Ramiros.

August 15. To UP Creative Writing Center: SV Epistola, Jimmy Abad, Franz Arcellana. Doding's driver, Ading, took us and Franz to PNB to get Franz's emeritus salary, then to Pepe Abueva, my Political Science professor, to give him copy of Gretchen's second book, *Negotiating Democracy*, University of Pittsburgh, 1996. The first was *Fragile Democracies*, University of Pittsburgh, 1995. We drove around the campus to see the changes since we were there last.

August 16. To the Commission on Culture, Manila Hotel.

August 19. To the Commission on Culture and Art in Intramuros.

August 20. Registered at Manila Hotel. Met Bernadette Churchill, former student of Len who had invited us to talk at the Centennial.

Room with view of Manila Bay. Supper with Frankie and Tessie Jose. Then see Father James Donelan and Father Joseph Galdon at Ateneo, Gloria Rodriguez at Giraffe.

August 2. Breakfast at Champagne Room with delegates. Len in a barong.

Fiesta Pavilion. President Fidel Ramos late.

Shuttle to Luneta for wreath-laying 5:20 p.m. Malaysian delegate, Roxy Roxas Lim, Nieves Epistola, Esther Pacheco.

Reception semi-formal. Met UP Law Professor Enrique Fernando, after forty years; Connie Alaras.

August 22. Breakfast 6:30 a.m. John Larkin panel. He asked me to translate a poem for his book. Press coverage, minimal. Mexican star getting all the attention.

Frankie and Tessie Jose treated to Kamayan lunch.

Reception, Fiesta Pavilion. Len's talk. Met the Epistolas, Karina Bolasco.

Cocktails. Farewell dinner. Len enjoyed meeting writer friends.

August 25. Went to see Sister Teresa at the Carmelite Monastery, with Virgie Moreno, Fel and Tess Santa Maria,

Amel Bonifacio and Amy, Andy Cruz. Reception with the Sisters. Father Gonzalez, NVM son, celebrated Mass. It was the last time Len would see all of them.

August 27. Brought the flowers to Mom and Dad at Himlayan.

August 30. Back in Boston.

2002 – ATENEO LIBRARY
OF WOMEN'S WRITINGS (ALIWW)

November 4, ALIWW. Rica Bolipata called about the award. Asked her to invite Fel and Tess Santa Maria, Rose Juan Bautista, Fr. Joseph Galdon, Josie Lacson. Sr. Teresa called. Len called. He and Gretchen received ALIWW invitations. He said, to make sure someone took pictures of "my moment." Invited Elma Unson Dizon, Judge Nene Abiog Magno, Hermy Abejo, UP Law classmates; and Br. Francisco Tanega, Br. Reh Vasquez; SOM.

November 8, ALIWW ribbon-cutting.

November 11, Monday. Edna Manlapaz called twice. Rica Bolipata arranged for my ride to the Friday program with the students at the Writing Center.

November 12, Tuesday. Opening of two-week ALIWW Library exhibit of my works: 3 p.m.

November 13, Wednesday. Parangal 4:30 p.m., in Audio Visual Room of Social Science building. Elma saved seats. The Award was given in the name of Virginia Licuanan who was a gracious presence. Gloria Rodriguez was honored as a publisher—she was director of New Day until she started Giraffe which published widely, including my books and Len's novel, *The Circular Firing Squad*. She does all the formatting, proofreading. Each time she and Ralph visited Cindy and Dan Militar in Connecticut, they dropped by to see us.

Gloria presented me with the first copy of *Stranded Whale*, dedicated to Franz Arcellana, Len, Luisa Garcia who introduced me to the computer. I gave a signed copy to Emy Arcellana who came with Beth. We had been friends for years. I remember exchanging visits the years we were neighbors in Area 17, UP, and I wished Franz had been there. Ma. Teresa Martinez Sicat said *Stranded Whale* allows us to witness the birth of our nation that had been fought for, over a hundred years ago. I put aside the response I had prepared since I had just written it. Rica Bolipata said, "You spoke so well, Ma'am. No palabas or performance." Wore brown and black Adrienne Pappell outfit that kind of matched Ma. Teresa's gown. Nadine told me Mila Aguilar said, "In person Linda was quite a surprise to me. So fine and pretty. She doesn't look her age. 71!"

A lot of students. Br. Francisco of Sons of Mary with Br. Reh Vasquez, Virgie Moreno. Met Carol Nunez who had reviewed *A Small Party in a Garden*, Joy Dayrit, Angel Eufemia of Library Consortium. Narita Gonzales, Fel and Tess. Reception: Philippine merienda which I enjoyed immensely. Since my sister and her husband had another engagement, Narita and NVM Gonzalez gave the night's dinner for me, inviting several writers. Then NVM and Jimmy Abad took me to Marikina. I remember potholes in the dark Dao Road.

November 15, Friday. 4:30 p.m. Ateneo Creative Writing Center. Language has to be both precise and ambiguous; a balance. Benilda Santos and students. Very good questions. Two hours. Benilda, Danton Remoto, and Rica were in the class Fr. Galdon asked me to hold at Ateneo, having me picked up at Araneta each afternoon. Felice Sta. Maria sent me Philippine American Literary House (PALH) report on ALIWW. Edna Manlapaz called. Rica told her that Friday with the students was a "graced" moment. Brought the ALIWW bouquet to Himlayan for Mom and Dad.

2003

April 9. University of Connecticut Cultural Center Reading, at the invitation of Roger Buckley. About 50 students, faculty attended. Dinner at the Cultural Center. There were friendly exchanges of ideas and books, discussions about future conferences. Good questions. Book Club members attended. Some said I am a "difficult read" but worth it. A student brought "The Other Side" article and short story. Len drove in the fog and rain. Roger said they'd invite me again.

April 22. Boston College. Filipino Authors Night. Reading, book signing. 7:30 p.m. Alberto Florentino also spoke. Met Ricco Siasoco, Grace Talusan, and BC students, Higgins Hall.

April 25. LA Festival of Books. 6-9 p.m. Gave signed copy of *The Stranded Whale* to Consul Helen Barber. An actor read the two Mullis chapters. Many writers came, many UP students; Law classmate Alberto Mendoza. Met Robert Little. Book signing. Other author was Tess Uriza Holthe, *When the Elephants Dance.* Gretchen joined us from Texas.

April 26. UCLA 2-4 p.m. Linda Nietes invited Len and me to the program at the Consulate where I gave a short talk and met Mr. Montifar-Samonte who designed the cover for *The Peninsulars.* He explained the process where he engaged his students and chose the final cover from the students' entries.

May 1. A reading at American River College in Sacramento with students and faculty; at the invitation of Patrice Gibson, chair of the Anthropology department.

August 9. Pamana Award. San Francisco/LA Action Theater: Program and Presentation. Met Luz de Leon and organizers, other writers.

Parade from Mission Street to Yerba Buena Gardens. Food booths. Len and Tina enjoyed afternoon. Truly Filipino. (July 8. Pamana Invitation from Luz de Leon: *I found you in a simple email and for many days, I read and reread your essay. It was "Tadhana." You gave so much validation to the work we do at Pistahan. Thank you.*)

In between those years I took part in the UP workshop. One year the resident fictionist from the US was unable to come, and when I showed up to visit, Franz asked if I would be staying long enough to take the writer's place. We stayed long enough to be invited by Virgie Moreno to Los Indios Bravos where writers spend the evening. I remember the black light in the Naughty Room. Len enjoyed meeting again so many writers he had met before. Bencab, based in London, was there one night. Sherman Carroll of Readers International used his paintings in the covers of *Awaiting Trespass*, and *Wings of Stone*.

Writer friends asked me to join them in conferences. Cecilia Brainard invited me to join her in the University of Connecticut program. I was asked to speak at the Texas A&M where Gretchen taught political science. Winnie Torres invited me to speak at MIT, (Institute of International Affairs) with Sonny Alvarez on the panel. Always it was a chance to connect with students and talk about our literature. I talked at local libraries to let people know there is a Philippine literature. Framingham State asked me to give a talk a couple of times, readings; and conferred on me an honorary degree, Doctor of Letters--May 2004--when Helen Heineman was president.

Catalina Velasquez-Ty (Linda Ty-Casper's Mother)

Francisco Figueroa-Ty (Linda Ty-Casper's father)

PART 3

ENDINGS

GABRIELA PAEZ VIARDO DE VELASQUEZ
1871-1953

Nanay's was the first death I remember. August 13. I came home from UP to find her waiting for me so she could be brought to St. Luke Hospital. Kuya Bebeng, Dr. Bernabe Mendoza, lived across from us at Araneta, and after seeing Nanay, suggested she be taken to St. Luke's Hospital. There were no regular checkups then. One saw a doctor when one was sick. I had not realized Nanay was bleeding internally. She never complained.

Relatives came to visit her at St. Luke's where she was confined after a blood transfusion. I would bring her an orange. Ninang told me afterward that the orange was too sour but she ate it, because I brought it. The transfusion did not work. It flowed out of her. I ran down Magdalena Street to the church and asked the priest to bless her. She was waked at home, though recently her sister, Lola Kikay was waked in Manila where the family brought her from San Isidro. The saya she wore was the one Nanay was saving for herself.

Nanay was interred in the cemetery of San Bartolome where, because she was a Paez, no fees were charged. I recall, Tio Uling Policarpio, Tio Osong Velasquez standing with my father in the living room where the funeral parlor had installed the lights. Neighbors and family came day and night.

I remember Lola Colasa, Nanay's sister-in-law. She was brought to the house since she was living alone. I remember her daughter Felisa who looked like Tia Pinang and had a son. Lola Colasa was quiet, merely smiled in answer. I remember her and Nanay listening to *Tawag ng Tadhana* on the radio, sharing a drink of sarsaparilla into which a raw egg had been beaten. She had no ailments but she passed away two days after Nanay, willing herself … I remember my mother coming to UP, to tell me. 1953. August 15.

FIDELA VELASQUEZ
1896-1980

On February 6, I learned Ninang had slipped and broken a hip. Baby, with whom she lived, entrusted her care to Ate Remy and Tia Mameng in Novaliches. She passed away in less than two weeks. I was not able to come home for her. After my hip dislocations, I realized how much in pain she had been, without the interventions of medical and nursing care that I had.

I remember her sewing dresses for Baby and me; in the kitchen cooking meals, so tired afterwards, that she went upstairs to her room to rest, instead of joining us. The few times she left the house was to have her eyes checked, going by taxi until we got a car. Then she came along while the driver took Baby and me to school, waiting for us in the back seat. Elegant chaperone. She made a snack for the driver but not for herself. I should have invited her to Little Quiapo for halo-halo which can be ordered regular or especial, and one can ask for more crushed ice and Carnation evaporated milk as one neared the bottom of the glass. I recall being told Ninang would open the box of candies and cookies I sent her from the States, to share with Baby's sons in Araneta, though I also sent them their own boxes; closing it again without taking anything for herself.

I remember her asking the man repairing the street to come in from the heat and have his tanghalian in the kitchen. Most likely she also served him what she cooked, adding to his baon. She did the same for men who repaired the roof after storms. She herself, however, rarely sat down with us to eat. Mostly, I recall her nibbling, instead of having a meal. She loved ice cream and pineapple, candies.

CATALINA VELASQUEZ-TY
1908-1982

Two years after Ninang passed away, March 22, Baby called: my mother was asking for me. She had retired from the Bureau and, had been working at the UP, on curriculum development, giving workshops in the provinces, as far as Abra, then suddenly had a stroke. Baby's husband was in the Philippine Army so they took Mom to V. Luna from the Railroad Hospital.

March 23. Had my passport stamped and got a sailing permit so I can reenter the US. Father John Morris started praying for Mom. Called Gretchen to let her know I'm leaving. Went from Boston, NY to Anchorage, to Seoul.

March 25. Arrived in Manila after 23 hours. Saw Mom, stayed with her in her room. She was feverish. Her room had no window curtains, no AC. She asked me to pray the rosary, and listened to me praying.

March 26. Second report: no malignancy in spinal fluid; liver scan suggested TB or cancer that has metastasized. Dr. Philip Ramiro suggested a brain scan.

March 27. Dad came by bus and jeep from Malabon. He insisted on paying for the medicine. Some are hard to get. Lirio and Ate Remy looked in several Merced drugstores. Then a knock at the door. A man said he was from the ward, heard my mother needed the medication his mother was on. "Mother does not need it any more. She just died." He refused to be paid. I include him in my prayers, with the taxi driver who brought Mom home when she fainted at the bus stop near UP and the jeepney drivers who brought Tia Pinang to Araneta when she was injured on her way home from Dasmariñas.

March 28, Sunday. Visitors: Bella, Stella, Ate Mameng, Tio During and Tia Nene Viardo, Marcia and Noel, Titong, Virgie, Gloria, Farrah. Tio Miling and Tia Angeling Viardo. Toning and Milagring Sabarre. Tomorrow, Dad and I will go to lunch, then I will see Tia Pinang.

March 30. AFP ambulance to Makati Medical Center for CT scan. Renald held dextrose drip. Tino brought Mom's blood sample to PGH and Capitol Center. Eddie de Vera came. Didn't have supper. Too tired.

April 1. Dr. Ramiro said there is no malignancy in brain or liver: wait 2-3 weeks before liver scan; don't agree to brain surgery.

April 2. Intern had trouble reinserting nose tube. Alpha-feta blood test—no primary hepatoma in liver. Good sign. Ate Remy came.

April 3. Doctors' round—biopsy, liver scan and ultrasound suggested.

April 4. Leni, Doding's niece, brought ice cubes for Mom to suck on. Too hot in room. Still no window curtains against the sun, no AC.

April 5. Dad brought Len's letter. Med tech unable to draw blood. Mom's finger pricked. Mom liked the massage and arm therapy. Masarap. She fell asleep during visiting hours: Father Froilan. Sebio and George de Vera brought fruits.

April 6. Mom asked for her things from the house. We have not found her diamonds. Relatives who came to the house said the maids were wearing Mom's clothes. Did they also find the jewels she kept in the pockets?

April 7. Mom had some feeling on left side. Left leg responding to Moriamin. We cheer when she takes her medicine by mouth. Is she getting better? More aware, Mom said, "I hope Len understands why you have to be here."

April 8. Mom pulled out her nose tube. Gina started feeding her by mouth. Mom doesn't realize she is paralyzed, wants to go to the bathroom. Mom insists on getting up, on walking. Dra. Tuazon: Mom has cysts in liver, but problem is really the stroke. Eddie said he had visited her at the Rail Road hospital and Tia Mameng had covered Mom's face with a handkerchief due to the facial paralysis from the stroke. Visited churches on Cavite, Rosario and Paranaque, while Mom slept.

April 9. I thought Mom died, 2:30 p.m. She asked to be held tight: "Ang buhay ko ay nasa langit." Earlier she had refused to eat. "Ayoko, ayoko, ayoko!" Dextrose, nose tube, catheter replaced. It took hours. She must be in pain, uncomfortable. General and Mrs. Santos, Lut Jamlig, Beatriz and Kit came.

April 10. Dad came, asked if I needed money for medicine. Violy brought caimito.

April 11, Sunday. Washed Mom with warm water. She woke up. She had been asleep since midnight yesterday. Not responding. Drs. Mapanao and Khian. Mass. Renald came. Dad came.

April 12. Called Len collect. Told him and Tina that Mom was in a coma yesterday. He said to stay as long as I need. Mom had trouble breathing. Resident came. Hermy brought papaya. Her birthday tomorrow.

April 13. Mom felt very cold. Called intern and nurses. No blood pressure. She was given Docard and Argumet, artificial respiration. I called Baby and Dad. ICU equipment brought to Mom's room. George and Eddie came.

April 14. Mom can't talk. The suction machine brings up blood. Can we not stop the treatment? Doctor suggests a cut-down. I don't know. X-ray brought to room. Talked to doctors. Ate Remy came. Now, I know that those interventions prolong not life, but dying. I should have said, NO.

April 15, Thursday. Mom died 9:15 a.m. before Dad arrived. I kissed her. The tubes were removed. Bet wiped her face with oil. I asked Baby to come in. She had stopped at the door. Ninang Trining and Ninong Benigno Marino came. I place her favorite flowered sheet over her, asked George to stay with her. Then, I called Len.

I had been sleeping in the hospital room with Mom, leaving only to attend the Pabasa at Tio Uling Policarpio, to go to the bank with Dad. Often, Mom asked me to say the rosary, listening while I prayed. I took each day as it came, praying. Only much later did I realize the toll of extraordinary measures—a cut in the ankle to check blood pressure, a food tube, tests of one kind or another—which I could have refused for her, to spare her needless pain. I thought they would somehow make her well. Through my fault, Mom did not have a painless passing.

At Loyola for the wake, I felt numb. Nene Abiog and Hermy Abejo had Mass for Mom. Fr. James Donelan of Ateneo, who came often to Araneta and also to Framingham, celebrated Mass. Many came. Dr. Dalmacio Martin chief of the Curriculum Division, Fred and Belen Morales, Mauro Avena, Tess and Frankie Jose. About fifty, relatives and friends were at Mom's funeral. Luz Villamor was there; the Syjucos and Viardos.

Interment at Himlayan. Fr. Jim Donelan celebrated Mass at 1 p.m. A man came, said he read she was an educator so he wanted to pay his respects. Padasal was at Araneta. Dad looks very tired. On doctor's orders Baby rested. Ate Amparing Mendoza, Ate Felisa San Gabriel, General and Mrs. Santos. Tia Pinang. Tia Trining and Tio Valentin. Bella and Michael. Aling Enyang led us in the Pabasa.

We had Mass at San Gabriel, on Araneta. Gregorian Mass, for 30 days. Dad and I get the lapida in Quiapo. Eddie and Lita, George and Lina invited us to Mass in Arayat, at the Church of Santa Catalina. Masses celebrated at Santa Scholastica; Concepcion church in Marikina.

April 30. Mom's birthday. Salo-salo in Araneta. Ate Remy. Called Len, I will have to stay to get the birth, marriage certificates, cedula, assignment papers and other documents for the extrajudicial partition; to check the bank accounts to protect Dad. A cousin of Dad came to remind him to share in the extrajudicial partition. I told him I am not looking for a share. In fact, when Mom and Dad told me the Araneta property was for me I didn't ask them to write it down. So, when the house was sold after Dad passed, some relatives took even my share of the sale. I had sold my only lot, for which Len started monthly payments, to cover Dad's expenses. I don't know what happened to his account. Nanay would have been appalled.

When I was cleaning Mom's room I found her sonnets, written on index cards. I typed them in the porch where she loved to sit, put them together for printing. Renald did the line drawings. I have two copies left of *Alone, With Each Other* which we gave to friends at the Philippine Normal College where a memorial was held. There were tears, ours and those who came to celebrate her life. Dad preferred Mom's book of sonnets to anything I wrote.

I returned home the day after Dad's birthday, on June 16. Dad went to Mass by himself, at San Gabriel, avoiding the fuss. In the afternoon we went to Himlayan, brought flowers and candles to Mom. He said, "After you leave, I will have no one to talk to." But he didn't want to go to the States with me. He didn't want to leave the house he built in 1941, in the rice fields where Revolucionarios waited to resume fighting.

In the plane, flying back, I remembered how simple things made Mom happy. On Saturdays, she enjoyed fresh lumpia in Divisoria, asking the man who sold it from his pails on the sidewalk for more garlic or peanuts; biting into the roll with the juices running all over her hand, over the diamond rings. Then she would ask for a box of six to bring home. No 5-star hotels for her. No showing off. I remember Nanay saying how Mom, when she was a little girl, wrapped herself about Nanay's knees when a dog rushed to attack them .... Those memories are the inheritance I treasure.

AGRIFINA VELASQUEZ
1897-1989

A few days after I arrived and all the pasalubongs—calculators, games, candies, perfume, shirts, dollars, cold cuts, etc.—were distributed, I was summoned at night to see Tia Pinang in Acacia where I had asked relatives to look after her. I had seen her as soon as I arrived, and was surprised she now looked so weak.

She was alone in her room. The family was having supper. I asked for warm water so I could wash her before, that same night, taking her to the Rail Road hospital. I stayed with her that night. Remembering Mom's hot clammy room at V. Luna, later, I asked for a room with windows. Ate Remy and I could not stay with her, since Dad was alone in Araneta, so I asked Tia Mameng to be with her. She said I should pay for private care for Tia Pinang.

The room was large. Airy. No one offered to bring her meals, so I arranged for the woman who sold food in fiambreras to provide them. Lirio, Ate Remy's daughter, brought Tia Pinang beef broth, washed her. It turned out, that relatives, meantime, were clearing her room. They burned her clothes and my letters to her, but did not find in a tin can the money I sent Tia Pinang every month. Lirio found it; and gave it to me. It paid for the hospital and doctors. A relative said no one paid hospital bills in a lump sum; asked why a private room?

Tia Pinang was scheduled to go home, but she died 6 a.m., February 15. She was waked at Our Lady of Grace church near the Bonifacio monument. An Oblate priest from Colorado blessed her, celebrated Mass. Joy and Iris read. Tia Pinang was buried with Nanay in the cemetery of San Bartolome church. Because she was also a Paez, as Nanay, no fees were charged. Our mercy meal afterward was at Ate Cording, in the Farmacia of Tio During. Those who should have cared for her did not come to the padasal and patapos. My friends Beatriz and Nene came, also the Policarpios. Bella sent mamon to Araneta. No one thought of saving any for Dad.

Among my regrets, I failed to honor Tia Pinang's wish: huwag mong ipakita sa kanila ang aking bangkay. I did not think of a closed casket when we placed her before the altar of Our Lady of Grace. Tia Pinang was beautiful, had many suitors. I could find no photograph of her to enclose in the thank you cards to those who had Masses for her.

FRANCISCO FIGUEROA-TY
1907-1990

My sister, Baby, called that Dad needed oxygen, and a nebulizer was expensive so I should bring one. I called Dad, but he only asked, "When you come, bring me a pair of black Florsheim." When I arrived, it was clear he needed to go to the hospital but he refused, so I urged him, "Let's go so you can wear your Florsheim." Only then did he agree to see his doctor, get checked at the hospital; stay for a day, maybe. He agreed, but he asked me to put the Florsheim where he could see it from his bed.

Dad had a large room with windows all around so he asked if we were in a hotel. The bathroom had hot water. We had a refrigerator. It was not Mom's room at V. Luna. Learning from that, each time Dad had to be confined, I insisted on a large, airy room. At the Heart Center there was a kind of long porch outside his door. At the Lung Center visitors had space to talk to each other and bring Dad meals from restaurants.

Dr. Messina was the admitting doctor at the Kidney Institute. Dr. Chavez, Dad's attending physician. Dad looked so weak. He slept off and on. Dr. Chavez, Dr. Dangilan, and Dr. Ramiro came to see Dad almost every day; sometimes returning later. They were trying to figure how Dad can breathe normally before and after an attack. Dr. Clarence Rasul, the son of my classmate at UP Law, Jainal Rasul, checked on Dad who continued to fight to go home, pulling his catheter and the tube implanted to drain the air trapped in his left lung. Dr. Danguilan reinserted them each time. The nebulizer was in constant use. The X-ray machine was brought to Dad's room. He needed a blood transfusion. There was internal bleeding. Dr. Danguilan came and offered to help clean Dad. I asked if Dad will get better. He said, "Anything can happen." The Staff at the Kidney Institute was good to Dad. They stopped to see him when they arrived, and before they left. One aide brought Dad an egg crate mattress he found in another room. "Lolo will be comfortable on this," he said.

Ate Remy and Lirio took turns at the hospital so I was able to leave Dad for quick trips to bring Len's manuscript to his publisher, get Len the books he wanted; to deliver the padalas, see the Sons of Mary, who visited Dad. Fr. John Wallace blessed and anointed Dad. On Ash Wednesday, Br. George Hungerman brought Ashes. When Dad was sleeping, I took a walk in the courtyard, attended Mass at the chapel, wrote Gretchen, Len and Tina. Sometimes. Dad would ask me to have the caro of the Assumption wait for him, dreaming perhaps of processions in Calibiga. Or ask me to look for the children of those who had been good to him when he was growing up.

Dad slept in the morning, was restless at night. He looked so alone. I had snacks with him when he was awake.

He still liked ice cream, but will only chew, not swallow even Max fried chicken. Sent for lanzones for Dad and the Nurses' station; pastries for Louise, Delia, Melissa, Abner, Joseph, Marian, Luz who came when Dad needed help. Dr. Meris prescribed Cicatrim for the bedsores. Water is a problem in Araneta. So, I asked Baby if Dad can stay in Marikina when he comes home. Nene Abiog and Candy came to see Dad. Feast of St. Blaise. Elma and Hermy called. We got a discount from the Billings department. Dr. Chavez and Dr. Danguilan charged very little for 46 days care. My bank account was down to half, but could still cover future expenses. I left the proceeds of the sale of my one property for his expenses, in order to keep his bank account intact.

I arrived January 16 in Araneta, my return ticket was March 6. I told Dad I was going to see Gretchen and Tina, would be right back. But he passed away early next morning, March 7. Fr. John Murphy of the Sons of Mary said that Dad waited for me to leave. His own father had. He grew up in the Mission Hill area of Boston. I learned, later, that the morning I left, Dad was moved to a smaller room, the window facing a wall.

I should not have left. I booked a flight back to Manila two days after I returned to the States. Melody and Manny met me at MIA. Dad was waked at Loyola, in the same room as Mom, eight years before. Frankie Jose and Tess were first at the wake, with Mauro Avena. Flory Orendain sent flowers. Fr. John Wallace, SOM, celebrated Mass also at the Carmelite Monastery with Sr. Teresa. The people who came at night to ask Dad for money, who stole his gun and clothes, never paid their respects. His own friends had passed, Mr. Santos, the year Mom died. Classmates from UP Law came. Purificacion

Parenas from grade school; along with the Muros, Toning and Milagring Sabarre.

CARMEN VELASQUEZ RAMOS
1898-1993

I arrived to find her no longer eating. I suggested leche flan but no one was able to make it. She sat under the trees in Marikina, sunlight flickering over her. When she recognized me, she began talking in English, asked about Gretchen and Tina. The maid said Tia Mameng ate when I fed her. Ate Luz de Vera came from Acacia to stay with Tia Mameng in Baby's house. We talked during our watch. It was like a wake. I limited accepting friends' invitations. My stay was too short. Only essentials: check the Banco de Oro account, go to BIR and to Ateneo re Len's books; meet NVM, Jimmy Abad, Esther Pacheco. Quick lunch at the Abejos to bring pasalubongs; then to the Sons of Mary to bring the padalas; go to Himlayan to bring flowers to Mom.

Tia Mameng did not complain, lay quietly in the shade until she was brought inside. She and Ate Luz had the room where the drivers used to stay. It had not yet been decided if she would be brought to the hospital. Her rehab schedule:

exercise, conversations to retain memory, turning her over to relieve bed sores. Ate Remy came with Jhona, Mayette and Bessie. Relatives came to celebrate Baby and Doding's anniversary. The children fished for tilapia in the swimming pool.

Too tired to go out. Just stayed with Tia Mameng. I kept remembering Dad saying I'm sintonado, because Tia Mameng taught me to sing, "I have a ball. A bouncing ball ..." in a monotone. I tried to remember her singing. As a child I had watched her being baptized into the Iglesia ni Cristo; recalled her asking me about the dab of ashes I received on Ash Wednesday—did she have no memory of growing up Catholic? She had been living in Araneta where she catered to her visiting children and grandchildren, often forgetting Dad lived there, too. Was her memory at risk then?

Tia Mameng was asleep the morning I left. It was decided not to wake her up. I thought of her during the flight home. I thought of all those, over the years, that I have had to leave. There is no easy way to leave.

Front, l-r: Neighbor, Linda Ty-Casper
Back, l-r: Linda's sister Baby, her Ate Luz, and her mother

AND...

Long before 2007 when I had the first of four joint replacements, knees and hips, at New England Baptist Hospital, I had pain in the joints, had to use canes and get injections from Dr. Eileen Winston. I was at Vigil to save St. Jeremiah from being closed, when a parishioner opened his laptop to the orthopedic section of New England Baptist. He said, "If you need surgery, this is a good list of surgeons." We crowded together, sitting in the vestibule, to read the write-ups about each specialist. At the end, Wayne Larkin asked, "Did you find any?" "The one who looks wholesome," I replied. An ER nurse, he said, "That's not how you choose a doctor," but Dr. Stephen Murphy was the right choice. When the nurse checked the dressing of the first hip surgery, she said, "That's the smallest incision I have seen." My last surgery with Dr. Murphy was 2017. He has checked each hip dislocation afterward. Now, Dr. Ana M. Navarro Espila from Spain takes care of me.

Len and I also developed macular degeneration. For years Len brought a church friend to Mass General for treatment but didn't realize he had developed it, too. I was seeing Dr. Felipe Tolentino whose reputation grew after he successfully treated an Austrian official, and after seeing me, Fel offered to check Len's vision even without an appointment. Len said he'd wait until school ended. By that time, the blank spot he described as a Neanderthal, had become dense. Laser left scars that further reduced his vision.

There were other surgeries for Len. One time, when NVM and Narita were in Cambridge, I took them to Wayside Inn, then to visit with Len who was recovering at home. From surgery. It was the last time we were all together.

We settled to a quiet life. Len loved living along the river. So many different kinds of green, he said, pointing to the shrubs and hydrangeas, butterfly bushes, white loosestrife, perennials that come up each year. Shoots from the nine lilies of the valley that came from Ruth McAleer quickly covered the slope to the river.

We enjoyed the summer my father and mother came, after retiring. My mother welcomed needed rest from attending conferences in Southeast Asia, holding workshops as far north as Bangued, where an impressed relative said she spoke without notes. After retiring from the Bureau of Education, she joined INNOTECH in UP working on a population study. That special summer, Len took them to historic places. Dad particularly enjoyed Concord. He could still recite William Wordsworth's poems, learned from the first American teachers. They enjoyed the Freedom Trail, Faneuil Hall, museums and historic houses like, Paul Revere's. Dad enjoyed the history he had learned. We went to Rhode Island, Maine and Connecticut, as well as Massachusetts. We visited friends, neighbors invited them over. They enjoyed Sudbury River and the backyard. They returned through Europe, thinking of the Holy Land next.

Len retired from Boston College in 1999, but began teaching at the Federal Program: Seniors teaching Seniors in

Wellesley on the suggestion of Al Duhamel who taught there after his own retirement. After some five years, Len had to retire a second time. But he continued to attend Boston College functions with Dan McCue, John Fitzgerald, Joe Longo. We exchanged dinners with the English faculty, and those from other departments. At that time, I had the energy to cook two chicken rellenos with all the trimmings, bake desserts as well. Sans rival was a favorite. I modified the recipe to have 14 layers. Mabini Castro said, "From now on I will eat only this cake."

Len joined the Methodist choir and was part of their annual musicals. He also joined the Coffee House Choir, while also with the Iskwelahang Filipino group where he sang bass with Mabini Castro, Ray Endriga and Bert Abriams. Raul Manglapus often accompanied Len when he sang solo.

Then, driving home one day Len lost his way, forgot where he was. Fel suggested a neurologist from Mass General. Finally, Len got an appointment with Dr. Thomas Byrne, who had treated Robert Penn Warren at Yale Medical. Talk about Nanay saying, years and years ago, that if it's meant to happen, it will. It's not coincidence.

For almost 16 years I drove Len to Mass General for the appointments, and check-ups; until he became eligible for the MBTA RIDE. Len and Dr. Byrne talked about conscience, consciousness, belief, and Robert Penn Warren. Len gave Dr. Byrne a copy of his second book on Robert Penn Warren— *The Blood-Marriage of Earth and Sky*—of which, James H. Justus said, "It is ethical criticism of a very high order."

While seeing Dr. Byrne, Len also joined the Callahan Center's Alzheimer group, Continuing Connection, which Lisa Ushkurnis directed. Eight couples met every Friday for four-five hours. There were movies, pet therapy, music therapy, art therapy, and always a lot of home-baked goods. Len liked chair volleyball so much, that the others, tossed him the ball when they got it, giving up their turn. Despite his macular degeneration which had destroyed his central vision, Len somehow tossed the ball over the net. At cornhole, most of the time, he sank the bag perfectly.

The experience of each other, whether they recalled each other's name or not, was positive. Uncanny things happened. At the end of a session, one would hug Len and next meeting we find out he had transitioned to a nursing home. Did they have premonitions? Holding my hand while walking to the car, Len would say, "There are good people in there."

After we left Continuing Connections, Patty Osborne whose husband Joel was part of the group, would call to see if I needed a visit. She, Jayne Surro, Jane Brown, Carol Fellman, Lisa Ushkurnis, Jamie Jenkins came often. When Len passed, we had a Mercy Meal at Bella Costa, one of Len's favorite restaurants. The Continuing Connection group helped celebrate Len's life. Vincent and Nancy Mendoza held a late birthday celebration for Len. It was Nancy who arranged for home hospice for Len with Care Dimension of Concord.

Our life has been filled with many good people. Mario Agostinelli added a library and a porch facing the Sudbury River, charging at cost because he said, "teachers are not paid much." Len loved to stain and paint. Mario let him paint the ceilings, walls, and windows. Those were Len's favorite rooms in the house. We live in that porch from where we could see the river and the birds and the plants we added over the years. I remember I once took Gretchen to Dr. Charles Morgan in Ashland when I thought she had smallpox, it was an allergy to

Timothy grass. Dr. Morgan brought us home so I would not have to get a taxi back.

Len, diagnosed with "an overall intellect functioning at the superior range" often had moments of full recall and clarity. Between occasional rages and deepening silence, he wondered about our finances, reminded me to take care of myself. He would point to the river, at the flight of swans and blue herons and say, "God put us here." Tina recalls Len singing "Oh what a beautiful morning" and telling her God wrote the song for the backyard.

Sitting by the river, Len would whistle to the birds. He watched the muskrat swim by, young deer sun themselves on the lawn, wild turkeys fly from across the river; small birds nesting in the hemlocks and umbrella pine trees he had planted. In the porch we kept bird books to identify each new visitor. Besides sparrows there were robins and cardinals, warblers, buntings, juncos, goldfinches and siskins, evening grosbeaks, scarlet tanagers, wrens and orioles, titmice, hummingbirds, woodpeckers, blackbirds with red in the wings, and the chickadees. Now and then, a bald eagle. And in the river, mergansers, swans, geese and ducks, mallards, Harlequin ducks, herons. Once a pheasant flew from across the river to the apple tree. A cormorant was blown inland by a storm. Once, Len knew all their names.

On his 95th birthday, July 6, 2018, Len passed away in his sleep. Months later, in a box I found a photo of Len I had not seen before, and letters tightly folded. In some the ink had faded. After much thought and hesitation, I typed the letters: hunt and peck. In April 2022, Cecilia Brainard asked what I was doing. I said I was typing Len's letters. She asked to see them, then emailed back next day: she would publish them as Len's memoir. By August, having formatted the manuscript.

and having asked Ian Rosales Casocot to design the cover, she sent me back the finished memoir: *Will You Happen, Past the Silence, Through the Dark*. It was the question Len had posed in a letter to me.

Just today, June 8, 2024, Cecilia said she would publish my memoir—*Lives Remembered*. I trust and love her and I am grateful. I had told her the wife of a writer emailed that my generation is "dead or dying" which prompted me to return to the memoir I had started; before my eyesight gets worse, and Cecilia emailed right back, "If you should want PALH to do the non-Filipino edition, here I am." I emailed back, "I would be happy if PALH will do the memoir, it's not just about me, but about so many lives that became part of mine. So many good people." Cecilia replied: "It sounds lovely. And thank you for trusting PALH/me once again." Before I met Cecilia, I had met her mother, Mrs. Concepcion Cuenco Manguerra, a beautiful, gracious woman who had been Cebu's Carnival Queen in 1931. It was at Professor Consuelo Asis, UP Biology, Luz Villamor's sister.

Cecilia Brainard had also published *A River, One-Woman Deep*, in time for Len to read it. He said, one must read it with full attention. There are interested parties trying to republish my three novels, collectively known as the Martial Law Novels—*Awaiting Trespass, Wings of Stone*, and *A Small Party in a Garden*—to counter current political disinformation attempting to erase the years of Martial Law from our nation's memory. I remember Gloria (Gigi) Gonzalez who came from Riverside, California, to interview me for her research project, The *Word and World of Linda Ty-Casper: A Critical and Literary Anthology*. The last time she came was with her colleague Hendrik Maier, who admired the Sudbury River. Later, Gigi's husband Bey and daughter Cosette came to visit with us.

Now 93, I live alone, but I'm not isolated. Monthly visits from Gretchen and Tina, anchor my life. Gretchen took early retirement from Penn State to look after my care. Tina opted for online teaching at American River College so she can come when needed. Len and I are proud of both daughters' accomplishments. Gretchen received her Ph.D. in Political Science from Michigan University. Kristina, from UC Davis in Native American Studies.

Now, Gretchen and Tina stock the freezer, take me out on short trips and lunch, take me to medical appointments; secured the help of Keily Cabrera as caregiver and Lisa Polesello for help with the house. Gretchen keeps fresh flowers in vases. Tina calls from California, or emails. For this Mothers' Day they got me yellow lupines, pink and white Columbines, orange hot pokers to fill in the gaps in the front beds, among the pink coral bells from Gladys in Rhode Island, white coral bells from Gretchen's garden in State College, blue Russian sage, columbines, evening primrose, astilbes, monarda/beebalm, blue flax, Queen Anne's Lace, golden ladders, mystery plants from seeds birds drop in the garden.

Neighbors keep an eye on me. The time I dislocated my left hip, Mark and Shelley Gourley followed the ambulance to the hospital, took me home after my stay. They come when the computer falters, the smoke alarms fail. Julie Rundlett sends home-cooked meals, her lasagna and stuffed shells are terrific. Dave gave me his cell phone number in case I called when they were not home. Years before, Tina sat for Scott, Leslie, Jennie and Kerrie. Casey Jewell calls to see how I am doing. Her husband Mike and their sons shovel us out when we can get no one to come. Once when snow piled high on the roof, Mike came to rake the snow, before going to the office.

Other friends offer support and help. I have only to call. They keep me company through letters and cards, emails and phone calls. Visits from George de Vera's children, Iris, Ian and Illya; from Dave Casper, all the way from Wisconsin bring back memories of the family; as do emails and letters from Len's nieces Jan Willman and Karen Jung; nephew Scott Willman and his wife Sally, letters from Tom and Marcia Shank from Florida, John and James Silva from Hawaii. Emails from the children of Ate Luz—Elizabeth and Chen from London; from Jessie's children; from Ate Remy's in Novaliches—Lorie, Mayet, Jhona; Elma Unson Dizon and I talk regularly, remembering the UP in the '50s; nephews of friends Hermy Abejo, and Nene Abiog. Michael and Delina Sannicandro's daughters Marie and Elaine bring me pastries that Delina used to send. Sue McGann patiently gave me Physical Therapy during my three hip dislocations.

Edna Manlapaz, Jimmy Abad, Carol Nunez and her sister CY Ollero, Lynn Grow, the Sons of Mary keep in touch. Nilda Rimonte, who reviewed several of my books, sends videos of Greater Manila. Evelyn Mello, former kamajongera, calls. Gina Perry updates me with news of other friends. Cris Castro and I find comfort in comparing our aches and pains, recalling the morcon, relleno and special Filipino dishes we used to be able to make. Pacita Kendall and Nellie Walker, Dad's nieces, keep in touch. From Maryland, and before returning after family visits to Werner in New York and, to Kurt in Connecticut, Joe and Mona Dasbach's children Eric and Marlena took turns driving hours, this past Pentecost so we could see each other. Mona brought me a copy of her *Memoirs*, and of a portrait by Fernando Amorsolo of her paternal grandparents, which the national artist painted when he was in high school.

Living alone by the Sudbury, I remember the many—family, friends; even strangers here and in the Philippines—who became part of my life. In UP, a parent took Gretchen's photo when she was the Virgin Mary for their Christmas play, asked the teacher Josie Bunuan to make sure I got it. I treasure the memory it gives of the Nursery School in UP Diliman. Mom's officemate told me to choose any gift I wanted from a store. I chose a white swan vase. I was maybe twelve and did not think of the price but Mr. IV Mallari didn't even look at it. In Cebu, I bought a coin purse from a woman, purposely left before she could give me the change, but she looked all through the market, until she found me. And, Cipriano, who for years delivered my parents' mail, who after much hesitations, finally asked me if I could send him a mouthpiece for his clarinet so he could continue to play with a local band from Malabon. So little to ask.

So many have been good to us, enriching our lives. Cecilia Brainard continues to support my writing. Dorothy Connell, founder and editor of Readers International, keeps in touch. Roger Bresnahan gladly recommended me for grants. I recall he wrote Bellagio, that I was "A stunning writer, kind and considerate." He came several times to interview me in Araneta, and my parents enjoyed talking with him during lunch. NVM took *The Peninsular* manuscript to Bookmark so I would stop revising it. Alberto Florentino offered to publish my first stories, *The Transparent Sun*, in his Peso Book Series, and published the second collection, *The Secret Runner* in 1974, eleven years later. Margaret Hartley of *Southwest Review* and Al Duhamel, Len's Boston College colleague, Burton Raffel writer, poet and editor of *TriQuarterly*, NVM sent recommendations each time Len requested them.

When Syracuse University Libraries added to Len's Papers, Daniel Sarmiento, curator of the 20th Century to the Present, picked up the boxes to save me the trouble of having to mail them. He also asked if I would be interested in sending my own papers, so they would be together with Len's in the Special Collections.

In 2024, Mara Coson brought out a reprint of *The Three-Cornered Sun* (1974) as the second book published by her new Exploding Galaxies. She asked Manuel L. Quezon III to write the foreword. Mom would have been delighted. The former President was one of her all-time heroes; along with Jose Rizal, and Diosdado Macapagal.

I no longer have the energy be able to go back to the historical novels; to the American campaigns in Mindanao; but maybe Jainal's and Elias' children/grandchildren will write about the atrocities. There is the need to call attention to role of guerrillas and civilians in the liberation of the Philippines during World War II. There are still boxes of clippings, books on the War in an upstairs room.

I regret many things: being impatient, quick to anger, unable to sustain kindness. I think of the old man who asked the servidora at the Chinese store for the piece of ham left on the knife she used to slice pieces for Dad; who left quickly when she shook her head. I could have given him what I got for Dad. I remember Dr. Nepomuceno down the street from us in Araneta, who interpreted the X-ray I needed to go to the States.

From time to time, I remember the man who stood outside the door in Camarines, trembling, unable to speak or knock; my aunts afraid to let him in. He is in "The Outside Heart" where a little girl gives a mute beggar her earring. Alone with my thoughts, I remember the CCD class that met at the house every Monday. Karen and Kenny Regan, Steven Scardino, Kenny Scata, Jimmy Casale, Bobby Astopoveh, Stephen Fogarty. And, of course, Tina. The dining table could not accommodate those whose mothers asked to have their children in my class. Len led them in singing. After making a crèche and other class projects, they had cookies and milk or Coke and played in the backyard. I recall Kathy Hanson in the processions, Steven Scardino holding the flag with the crown of flowers. I remember Tina at four or five years old recognizing Father James Donelan sitting with us at dinner suddenly realizing he was a priest, asking him, "Why can't I see God? Does God walk or fly like the angels?" I remember Father Jim flew us with Gretchen to Ilocos Norte so we could see the beach there. The small plane hovered just over the tops of trees all the way to and back. He also took us to Lipa to see the church on the hill. And he celebrated the funeral Mass for my mother.

Now as Len did, I watch the swans, chickadees, sparrows, nuthatches, gold finches, cardinals, blue herons, wrens—many birds I can no longer name or hear—flying about the trees Len had planted in the backyard: quickly darting hummingbirds and goldfinch among the monardas, glory bowers, red pokers; plants from Rivers Edge Nursery, down river from us. Jennifer Potter and her father gave advice on pests, including tips to outsmart deer and rabbits.

When the hummingbirds and goldfinches flock to the bee balms/monardas, I remember family and friends gathered along the Sudbury River; Gretchen and Tina playing in the garden, planting and weeding along with me, skating on the Sudbury in the winter when ice was over a foot thick, throwing lettuce to the swans in the spring; yodeling in the back seat during car trips, Len planting hemlocks, butterfly bush, yews, dogwoods, red buds from Weston Nurseries, where in April Len took the girls to watch the Boston Marathon runners at the starting line; Mom and Dad sitting under the shade of red maples and dogwoods, red bud, and mountain ash, blue spruce, pines and birches, oaks—the good, happy years meant to last but are quickly gone—and I am able to start the day with a grateful heart.

*

This memoir is about the lives of all the people who have become a part of me and made me who I am. I am especially grateful to Gretchen for her manuscript edits and for Kristina for help with typing and photos.

~end~

THE AUTHOR

LINDA TY-CASPER'S short stories are a portrait of the country. "The character of their wisdom and strength give the stories their distinct nationality": Mauro Avena. They "must first be read as information, then as knowledge, which is power …" Franz Arcellana.

Her novels, both the historical and contemporary are set in critical periods in the fight for independence, freedom and justice. As information and knowledge, they preserve history from revision. Through both short stories and novels, the country becomes part of the story and history of the world.

She has received the SEA Write Award, the ALIWW Parangal, FAWN, among others. She had grants from Harvard, Radcliffe, Djerassi, Rockefeller/Bellagio. She's member of Boston Authors, UP Writers. She remains a citizen of the Philippines.

PRAISE

ALWAYS ENCOURAGING her readers to remember the past, historical novelist Linda Ty-Casper, now in her nineties, has gone on this journey for a final time through writing her own memoir. Recalling wartime moments to everyday appointments, she tenderly returns a whole cast of names and places to life, with family come and gone but all clear and warm as yesterday. Ty-Casper is hands down one of my favorite recorders of history for the way she materializes times lost to us, and she has accomplished this now with her own life. A must-read for fans of Linda Ty-Casper.

Mara Coson
Publisher of Exploding Galaxies

~

A LIFE WELL-LIVED. We hope to lay claim to this when we look back at our time spent on this stage called life.

For Linda Ty-Casper, foremost fictionist, the first Filipina writer in English who ventured into the difficult historical novel genre, it is now her own personal history she focuses the spotlight on. And a most interesting and rich life story it is. In her characteristic meticulously detailed narrative spanning some eighty years, she brings us to a world filled with a remarkable variety of encounters, of experiences with interlocking ties of family, friends, colleagues, fellow writers, neighbors, even strangers—people, she says, who have become a part of me and made me who I am."

So. Her *Memoir* seems, on the surface, as much about their lives, as it is, hers. From a childhood listening to a grandmother's stories of their lives during revolutionary times in the late 19th century and the American Colonial Occupation, and to years after, spent in the public school system, including the University of the Philippines Law School, capped by passing the Bar as one of those ranked high. She set off for more, in American universities which are among the oldest and most prestigious, and soon found writing, not the practice of law to be her true 'aficion' and her calling.

In a lifetime spent with literary critic Leonard Casper, Linda found a true kindred spirit who helped her nurture her passion. He was her patient but thorough behind-the-scenes editor and critic. She also carefully honed her craft formally, in writing programs and fellowships, as well as through her friendships with highly acclaimed fellow writers along the way. And rewards she reaped for the writing she would at times feel a bit guilty about, because it turned her away from being a lawyer.

This *Memoir* would be a companion piece to her literary fiction, for it is in both that the reader may glimpse at and be rewarded with insights on the writer's soul.

Today, in her later years, Linda Ty-Casper says, "I live alone, but I'm not isolated." Still, there are her daughters and their families, neighbors, countless friends she has kept in touch with through all these years, watching out for her.

And her recollections of an enviable life truly well-lived.

Thelma E. Arambulo,
Writer, Literary Studies Scholar
Former UP Chair
Dept. of English and Comparative Literature

~

LINDA TY-CASPER'S *Lives Remembered, A Memoir* is specifically, as she says, about "the lives of all the people who have become part of me and made me who I am," and she narrates her interactions with a remarkable number of people. In fact, in all respects the specificity of detail is remarkable. It's a Remembrance of Things Past that goes beyond Marcel Proust's A la Recherche du temps perdu. Readers are treated to an account of a life well-lived.

The book opens with a nostalgic depiction of 1930's Manila, an urban scene worthy of an Amorsolo painting. Immediately thereafter a short account of the bleakness and horror of the Japanese Occupation is juxtaposed. In the middle of the book is a rhapsodic landscape description with the poetic quality of a Jose Garcia Villa lyric like "Girl singing. Day." Scattered throughout *Lives Remembered* are a few insights into Ty-Casper's writing process and the origins of her stories. Although features like these and her stature as a first-rank author make this book a "must read" for literary critics, it is very accessible to anyone who fancies autobiographies and memoirs. *Lives Remembered* is a paradigm of inclusiveness of people, places, and events. Ty-Casper has kept her promise to her father never to give up her Philippine citizenship, yet most of this book is set in the United States and invokes American cultural features.

As Cecilia Manguerra Brainard has noted in the "Introduction" to her essay collection *Philippine Woman in America*, "I often feel as if I were straddling between two countries, two cultures … I married an American, had children, accumulated friends, memories and things …" *Lives Remembered* should be acquired by libraries in both countries as a welcome enrichment of literary history.

Lynn M. Grow, Ph.D.
Emeritus Senior Professor of English,
Broward College, Florida

~

LIVES REMEMBERED, A MEMOIR by Linda Ty-Casper chronicles a seemingly banal life that spans 90 years, starting joyfully in a relatively comfortable and loving extended family in Manila, punctuated by the horrors of the Second World War, followed by years of rebuilding a country in tatters. Eventually, she marries an American critic, Leonard Casper, and they raise a family in the US.

Ty-Casper recounts those years with her meticulous eye for details, sprinkling some Tagalog words and expressions here and there that give her narrative a distinct Filipino flavor.

Best known as a writer of historical fiction, Ty-Casper never dreamt of becoming one. She studied law at the University of the Philippines but while doing research at Harvard, she stumbled upon some documents denouncing the American occupation of the Philippines by US citizens themselves, and historical accounts that portrayed the Filipinos as helpless and willing subjects of an emerging colonial power.

Her passion for truth awakened in her the desire to set things right, not by writing history books, but through historical fiction based on research. At the same time, she recalled her maternal grandmother's constant plea that someone should write the untold stories of ordinary Filipinos under Spanish and American rule.

Ty-Casper realized that her training to become a lawyer had prepared her for this mission. She thinks her books are "briefs for the country, so [our] history will not be written for us: so we will be part of the world's story, not remain in the footnotes: the world can know and imagine us through our stories."

Readers who find Ty-Casper's historical novels will discover clues from *Lives Remembered* of how an author's life, particularly religion and family, shaped her writings. Yet more importantly, they will discover that humility of a writer who pursues and develops her talent at the service of her people. No, she does not regret giving up law practice. She thinks her classmates who practiced law and occupied key government positions made up for her decision to follow "the road not taken."

For someone who has been regarded as "underestimated and under rewarded," Ty-Casper proves that fidelity to one's art is its own reward.

Carol A. Nuñez, Ph.D.
Former Faculty Member,
Department of English, Ateneo de Manila University

From Linda Ty-Casper's Photo Album

179

MORE BOOKS BY PALH

(Philippine American Literary House – palhbooks.com)

Benedicta Takes Wing and Other Stories by Veronica Montes

Please, San Antonio! & Melisande in Puris (novellas) by Eve La Salle Caram and Cecilia Manguerra Brainard

A River, One-Woman Deep: Stories by Linda Ty-Casper

Will You Happen, Past the Silence, Through the Dark: Remembering Leonard Ralph Casper by Linda Ty-Casper

Anthologies

Asian and Philippine Folktales Retellings by PAWWA

Contemporary Fiction by Filipinos in America

Fiction by Filipinos in America

Fundamentals of Creative Writing, Revised and Expanded Edition

Growing Up Filipino: Stories for Young Adults

Growing Up Filipino II: More Stories for Young Adults

Growing Up Filipino 3: New Stories for Young Adults

Magnificat: Mama Mary's Pilgrim Sites

www.ingramcontent.com/pod-product-compliance
Lightning Source LLC
Chambersburg PA
CBHW022021090426
42739CB00006BA/231